(Un)Normalizing Education

Addressing Homophobia in Higher Education and K–12 Schools

(Un)Normalizing Education

Addressing Homophobia in Higher Education and K–12 Schools

by

Joseph R. Jones
Mercer University, Macon, Georgia

≡IAP

INFORMATION AGE PUBLISHING, INC.
Charlotte, NC • www.infoagepub.com

Library of Congress Cataloging-in-Publication Data

A CIP record for this book is available from the Library of Congress
http://www.loc.gov

ISBN: 978-1-62396-706-2 (Paperback)
      978-1-62396-707-9 (Hardcover)
      978-1-62396-708-6 (ebook)

CONTENTS

PREFACE

Addressing Homophobia in Higher Education and K–12 Schools

As children, we are taught, through social normalization, what behaviors are acceptable and necessary for us to "appropriately function" within society. Social normalization begins at birth and is a vicious cycle of acceptance and exclusion, one that exists in every aspect of society. If accepted and followed, socialization will confirm us a respected place within our community. If rejected, it will exclude us. Socialization includes every aspect of our lives, even sexuality. In terms of sexuality, society attempts to socialize individuals into accepting and functioning within a normative sexual ideology.

In order to truly conceptualize the role of social normalization, as it relates to sexuality, it is necessary to first briefly examine several aspects of normative sexual ideology: performance, reiteration and hegemony. In basic terms, performance is process through which individuals act in order to display an "accepted identity" for the dominant culture. Scholars, such as me, argue that gender and sexuality are repeated acts through which individuals engage to demonstrate a perceived identity for their community and the larger society. In doing so, sexuality is a set of constructed perceptions about what it means to be a sexual identity, not a reality. To that

(Un)normalizing Education:
Addressing Homophobia in Higher Education and K-12 Schools, pp. vii–xi
Copyright © 2014 by Information Age Publishing

end, performance connects to reiteration, which underpins the development of a constructed normalized sexual identity.

Reiteration is the process of engaging and displaying repetitive acts that depict for society an acceptable gender and sexuality. According to Leitch et al. (2001), "the little boy learns that his crying is not masculine; he must grow into his masculinity by imitating the behavior designated as "male" to the point that such behavior becomes "second nature" (p. 2486). It is through the process of reiteration that the little boy displays a socially normative and an appropriate gender and sexual identity to his community. Thus, because of the reiteration processes in society, there will always be established normative sexual identities. It is important to note that all of this happens because of hegemonic practices.

Hegemony is the power exerted by the dominant culture to control other individuals. It is the predominance of one belief and perception over another. According to Gramsci (1992) hegemony is the dominance of certain ideologies, practices, principles that are placed on other cultures for the purposes of controlling others. In addressing how hegemony influences sexual identity, Foucault's (1978) offers some insight concerning the notions of power regimes. Foucault argues that human beings are constantly engaging with a regime of power that wishes to regulate society's sexuality. Foucault believes that social institutions such as school, medicine, law, and religion govern sexuality and sexual desires through establishing categories that are continually placed in opposition to each other through discursive regimes. In discussing the history of sexuality, Foucault traces how society has marked certain sexual practices (masturbation, sodomy, adultery, etc.) as deviant from the norms of modern culture as established through social institutions. For example, he cites how schools separated young children to discuss their sexuality. In these same sex groups, the children are taught how to speak properly about sexuality in rigid and technical terms (Foucault, 1978). Thus, the institution of school engages in hegemonic practices by controlling the ways the children discuss and engage in sexual activity.

Further, Foucault uses the example of teachers in male boarding schools who aimed to produce acceptable behavior concerning masturbation. Foucault (1978) argues that through discussions of this sexual act by school officials, the nature of sexuality and sexual desires enters into regimes of power that label and categorize masturbation as anti-normative according to the teachers, who hold the power. The teachers controlled students' sexual acts through labeling something as anti-normal and inappropriate. Drawing on Foucault's discussions of power regimes and sexuality, scholars propose that one's community and a larger society dictate acceptable displays of sexuality. Therefore, the notions and beliefs about sexuality are constructed through an individual's normative socialization and society's regimes of power.

One space which society uses to perpetuate social norms and ideologies is during the process of schooling. Schools are places where children learn appropriate behavior beyond families. In many cases, schools are simply a reflection of the community in which the school is located. Thus, as children age, schools become the normalizing factor of children's lives. In schools, society's beliefs about others and anti-normative behaviors are solidified. It is through our educational practices that children learn what happens when someone is not "like" everyone else. In schools, children learn what happens to the "others" that exist in their communities. It is here that the binary oppositions of social normalization are further constructed and perpetuated.

Because of this, educators must recognize how binary oppositions function within schools and how they perpetuate society's heteronormativity within educational settings. A number of theorists suggest that all human beings are influenced by binary oppositions, such as good and bad, true and false, writing and speech, father and son, inside and outside, original and copy, and so forth. Binary oppositions are two opposing concepts that society have placed against each other in order to define each other. Because of the need to define concepts as they relate to other concepts, such oppositions will always exist. Thus, there will always be the contrasting notions good versus evil, male versus female, true versus false, and so forth, because we define something by juxtaposing it to what it is not; "it" versus "the other."

One such "other" within binary oppositions revolves around sexual identity. Our society has created schools that perpetuate heteronormativity by relying on the foundations of binaries. By heteronormativity, I mean a privileging of a heterosexual identity over all other identities by claiming that heterosexuality is normal and all other identities are anti-normal. In doing so, heteronormativity creates a binary opposition in which normal sexual identities (heterosexual) are viewed by schools as acceptable and anti-normal (non-heterosexual) are viewed as unacceptable. This binary opposition becomes the lens through which educators and educational institutions construct their understandings of sexual difference. Further, it is through this binary opposition that normative sexual identities are constructed and deemed as appropriate by members of the school community.

Heteronormativity is a powerful aspect of schooling and social normalization. It controls the treatment of students and school members. It controls curriculum and decision making. In some cases, it controls the hiring of faculty and staff. Therefore, it is imperative that we begin unnormalizing sexuality within our schools. By unnormalizing, I mean a process of breaking free from the structured definitional aspects of socialized normative sexual behavior. In essence, "un" normalizing involves a demystifying and deconstructing of the attributes of heteronormativity and how social normative ideologies perpetuate homophobia. Further, unnormalizing education is a process that seeks to dismantle the binary constructions surrounding sexual identity that exists in society and social normalization; thus, destroying the binaries that confine our cognitive functions concerning sexuality and sexual identity.

In order to dismantle binaries, we must recognize the superiority that binaries place within our thought and definitional processes. Because of social normalization, society understands and places superiority on straight because it is the opposite of gay. In the straight versus gay binary, society considers straight to be superior, or the more accepted form of sexuality. However, "you can't define or explain what heterosexuality is without doing so in relation to, and distinction from, homosexuality; heterosexuality therefore needs homosexuality to make any sense, even to exist at all" (Nowlan, 2008, p. 2). Therefore, a heterosexual sexual identity is not superior because in order for heterosexuality identities to exists, there must be non-heterosexual identities. Thus, one of the goals of unnormalizing education is to destroy the presumed superiority that exists in binary oppositions, and thereby establishing equality among the ways we view difference and otherness. In order to establish equality, we must begin exploring how the process of schooling becomes the catalyst through which performance, reiteration, hegemony and binaries continue to thrive in our school communities and the broader society.

It is because of the lack of equality and the role it plays in schooling that I have decided to pen this book and title it *(Un)normalizing Education*. As I argue in the first chapter, the problem of homophobia is rampant in our educational environments. When students are afraid to attend classes and are committing suicide, we must begin examining the role that heteronormativity plays in destroying safe schools for all students. This recognition provides a commencement point to begin unnormalizing education. In that capacity, it requires educators to recognize the problem because as researchers indicate, many educators do not believe that homophobia is a tremendous problem in "their" school. After conceptualizing the problem, unnormalizing education involves an unmasking of our true tolerance, which constitutes a realization of educators' true beliefs about non-heterosexual identities. Additionally, unnormalizing education involves educators at all levels to uncontextualize language and behaviors, to unraveling perceptions and to unsupporting the hierarchy of hate language, among other necessary steps.

Further, unnormalizing education requires all educators to remove their focus from the "gay kid" and how their schools treat the "gay kids," how the "gay kids" are dressed, or what language was used toward the "gay kid."

In doing so, their discussions should focus on the idea of "straightness" or what does it mean to be straight in their school. In doing so, teachers must begin to discuss how heterosexism and heterocentricity is reproduced in their schools through the ways that educators define and discuss homophobia. Through examining the notions of how educators mark "queerness" in their schools, educators will be able to explore the assumptions of how power functions in society and in schools. It is imperative that educators begin to recognize that power extends beyond dialogue, and exists within institutional structures. Thus, educators should examine how "straightness," rather than "queerness" operates within school environments; in doing so, it will create spaces to unnormalize education.

This text seeks to create a dialogic space, through which educators can enter into a discourse about the normalization of sexuality within schools. Its aim is to examine and explore how we, as educators, can begin disrupting heteronormativity and homophobia in our own educational settings. We must begin to unnormalize the social constructions of sexuality within our schools. In doing so, schools will become places where all identities are valued.

ACKNOWLEDGMENT

I would like to personally acknowledge Dr. Sandra Schneider for her help in constructing this work. I am thankful for the many academic conversations in which she and I engaged. Such conversations were catalysts for my own academic reflections. For those conversations, I am incredibly appreciative.

CHAPTER 1

(UN)DERSTANDING THE PROBLEM

If a kid was bleeding on the playground, you would attend to that. It's necessary to deal with that. In reading if a kid was stumbling across a word, you would help him sound out the word. You would involve yourself with them in a relationship. But, then the slurs come or something that has to do with gay issues and you just ignore it.

—Fran Steigerwald, PhD, LPC

Normative ideologies control the lenses through which a community views sexuality and sexual difference. Schools are reflections of the community in which they are situated; thus, schools become embracing institutions of normative ideologies. In doing so, schools are places where sexuality is examined through binary lenses of "accepted sexuality" and "non-accepted sexuality." As referenced in the preface, Foucault (1978) argues that through the treatment of sexuality, schools control the belief systems about sexuality and perpetuate a larger societal belief about sexuality and sexual identity. Therefore, in many ways, schools act as agencies through which heteronormative ideologies are thrust upon students and school personnel.

Because schools are agencies, I postulate that in order to unnormalize beliefs about sexuality in schools we must first recognize how heteronormativity functions within schools. In doing so, we must first understand the climate of schools and how those climates promote homophobic bullying.

(Un)normalizing Education:
Addressing Homophobia in Higher Education and K–12 Schools, pp. 1–10
Copyright © 2014 by Information Age Publishing

As a former high school English teacher, I daily observed the prejudice against gay and lesbian students. Many times throughout the day, I verbally addressed the hate language that some of my students endured in the hallway and the cafeteria by reprimanding students' language choices. Also, I attempted to address homophobia by discussing the lives of gay, lesbian, bisexual, transgender and questioning (GLBTQ) authors whom we were reading. As a teacher, I saw how homophobia affected the lives of gay and lesbian students

Yet, not all educators feel the same about homophobia and its prevalence in schools and universities. A number of educators do not believe that homophobia is a problem in their schools (Jones, 2010). Moreover, a number of school administrators deny the existence of homophobic bullying in their schools (Jones, 2011c). In fact, one teacher believed her principal was not willing to address it, "In my school, administrators do not want to deal with homophobia. They know it's a problem, but it's all about pretending it's not there" (Jones, 2011c, p. 20). However, the reality is that homophobia has reached epidemic proportions.

According to the 2003 National School Climate Survey by the Gay, Lesbian, Straight, Education Network (GLSEN), 84% of gay, lesbian, bisexual and transgender (GLBT) students experienced homophobic remarks or verbal harassment; of those, 91.5% reported hearing the words "[the F word]" or "dyke" on a regular basis, and more than 60 % felt unsafe in their schools because of their sexual orientation. Further, GLSEN (2008) also reports that to date these statistics have not changed significantly (Jones, 2011c).

In terms of homophobia in schools, the most recent National School Climate Survey also revealed that faculty or staff intervened in only 3.4% of the harassment cases. Furthermore, 36.5% of gay, lesbian, bisexual, transgender students reported skipping school at least once within the previous month because they felt unsafe in school (GLSEN, 2003). The study also revealed a negative correlation between harassment and the grade point averages of non-heterosexual students. Moreover, students who reported facing a great deal of harassment reported having no plans to attend college. Data examining schools argues that there is little change in the ways that students are treated in classrooms and schools (GLSEN, 2008).

Attached to this notion of distress, the media has reported that a number of students have committed suicide within the last year in the United States as a result of homophobic bullying. One student hanged himself; his parents were told that he was constantly bullied in schools because of his sexual orientation. Recently, there have been several "special reports" on bullying in schools by such people as Anderson Cooper and other national news journalists. Students are hurting themselves because of homophobic bullying. A new campaign, "It Gets Better," recently made national headlines as people such as Hilary Clinton, President Obama, and other national figures filmed themselves urging non-heterosexual youth to stay strong; indeed reminding them that "it does get better." Yet, the news stories attest to the reality that youth are still hurting themselves because of homophobic bullying.

The problem of homophobia in schools is more rampant than most people realize, and in order to unnormalize education, we must begin to truly conceptualize the power of homophobia in educational settings and the how social norms have created hostile schools. While conducting interviews, I spoke with college students and educators from higher education and K–12 schools from around the country. I have chosen to include some of their personal accounts of homophobia in their respective institutions. In doing so, I am not attempting to create a "victimization" mentality of non-heterosexual individuals. Rather, it is my aim to illuminate others' beliefs and provide a personal account about homophobia and heteronormativity and how it truly functions within our schools.

MADISON[1]

I met Madison approximately a year ago. He is a rugged young man who attends a local state university. He is only 20 years old. From our conversation, I deducted that he is quite bright. He has an incredible command of language and is very laconic. As our conversation developed he began to discuss his high school years. He grew up in the state in a middle class family; one where he was expected to attend college. His parents both worked outside of the home. His father was a small business owner and his mother a nurse. According to him his high school years were horrible. Although he had not come out in high school, everyone knew. They constantly harassed him, and he avoided sports because of the harassment and possible locker room assaults. He learned how to skip school without his parents finding out. However, his grades never suffered. He graduated with an incredibly high GPA. To him, high school was not about having fun, but rather it was about survival.

As we talked, he described the countless homophobic slurs that he heard on a daily basis. When asked, he could not remember one teacher or administrator who stopped the harassment. He describes his school as a predominantly White middle class community. As with his peers, he was able to drive his own car to school. For him, that was one the greatest days of his life because he no longer had to ride the bus, a place where enormous amounts of bullying took place. He could then control when he arrived and left school. Because of his new control, he was able to avoid the morning harassments by taking home his first period books. The next morning he would not have to stop at his locker; rather, he simply went to class just a few moments before the tardy bell sounded.

His second greatest moment in high school arrived when he was able to join the few students in his school selected for the college joint enrollment program. During his senior year, he took his remaining core courses at the local community college. He was able to gain the necessary credit and avoid the bullies who threatened him on the high school campus.

I asked Madison if college life was better. He replied, "Some. You still have all the words and see crap written on white boards in the dorm. But, here your friends seem to care more. They seem to take up for you if someone is being a jerk." Madison graduates soon and has plans to attend law school.

ROB

Rob is a 25 year old Caucasian male who works at a predominantly large Caucasian state university. He is tall with dark brown hair and brown eyes. He self-identified as a young gay male. His undergraduate degree is from a small liberal arts college in a nearby state. He returned home after school and accepted his current position. He has worked in higher education for one year and enjoys the atmosphere.

Although he loves his job, he does believe that there are enormous challenges on campus. As a member of the student affairs office on his campus, he is involved in the daily lives of students on campus. Every day, he hears some form of homophobic slur towards other students. He has also heard faculty and staff use the same hate language. He recalls how students write homophobic language on other students' white boards in the dorms and in the bathrooms across campus. He recalled the following story:

> I was walking across campus behind a guy on his cell phone. I was fairly close to him. He was also oblivious to the rest of the world. I heard him talking about a professor on campus. "I just left Dr. [insert the F word] class. He is so gay. I hate going to his class." The student continued to ramble on about how horrible this professor was. And, things like this happen all the time on campus.

When I asked him about his personal experiences, he recounted:

> I came out in high school. I should not have. It made my life horrible. I guess it was just not the right time socially to admit to anyone in school that I was gay. I think I was the only out gay kid there. My high school is right down the road. It is so socially conservative like most of the state. When I came out, it was tough. I went through the normal stuff, teasing, called a [F

word] and stuff. I went away to college in Virginia. It was a little better. But, the school I went to was known to be more opening and accepting. I met a lot of gay people. There was a gay/straight alliance. There was still a lot of homophobia but not as much as we have here.

For Madison and Rob, homophobia was and is still a tremendous challenge on their respective schools. Their stories are derived from my recollections of our discussions. Thus, they contain my own subjectivity. However, the following individuals are their own personal accounts of their schooling experiences.

JASON[2]

I grew up in a small town in Alabama. I was raised in a protestant home filled with love and support, except for the gay thing. I did not tell anyone in high school. And, to this day, only a sibling knows. I remember the harassment started in middle school. I was the kid that everyone picked on because everyone knew I was different. I knew I was different. I did not come out until I was a college junior, but even as a middle school student I knew I was gay. I tried to hide my sexuality by dating and attending the prom, but those were only superficial relationships that helped stop some of the harassment.

Sometimes, it was bad. I was targeted by bullies almost weekly. I was spat on, called a faggot, pushed into my locker, and many more things. I would tell teachers, but no one stepped in until it became physical. So, I stopped telling. I just avoided those people. Yet, the verbal assaults were just as bad for me. I must admit that it was only a few guys that picked on me the most. They were trouble makers and always caused problems. They picked on everyone about everything. But, I was very happy when they were suspended because that meant that I would get a reprieve for a few days. The only thing that really got me through high school was the peer groups that I had. I did have a great group of friends who always commented "what a jerk someone was" for calling me a faggot or queer. I was in show choir with most of my friends. I earned good grades and graduated with honors. I also swam on the swim team. I know they are very stereotypical gay things but they are things that I enjoyed. All of my close friends did them; so I did them.

But, I also remember just wanting to get out of high school. I hoped that college would be different than high school, and I wanted to go away where I could just start over. I graduated with several scholarships. I attended an out of state college where I joined an SGA group. This was a new experience because my high school did not have a group like this. I was not out and proud even in college, but I was happy. It was kinda weird. The harassment stopped in college. I was the same person just older. But, it was like all of a sudden everyone grew up, and kids were not mean anymore. Even as an adult, I am not harassed as much anymore. It may be that I have chosen to surround myself with people who don't really care about my sexuality. Who knows? But, it could also be that maybe society is changing. Or that people are only hiding their real feelings about gay people.

As a student and being "different," I wanted to be more than what those people thought. I always felt that I had to achieve more and be better at things. So, these guys, and it was always guys, were calling me a fag or something, and I was trying to get the highest grade. That also helped me through high school. Because, I knew that those guys may pick on me now, but if I could be more successful at things than they were, it would kinda validate me. But, I think that when you grow up in a hostile environment, you constantly have to perform. You have to continually prove that, "yeah I may be gay, but I am also successful in other areas of my life."

LISA

I have always been classified as a "lip-stick lesbian." In the lesbian community, this means that I act more feminine than other lesbians. I wear dresses, skirts, make-up, etc. I knew in high school that I was a lesbian, but I was more accepted because I was passable. I say this because I did not experience any abuse until I was outed by a teammate. It was during my junior year of high school, and I thought I could confide in one of my volleyball teammates. I thought that it would be okay. I told her that I had feelings for another girl. This turned out to be a huge mistake. I was immediately ostracized. My teammates all turned on me. It was not physical abuse. It was emotional abuse. I think that I would rather have someone hit me or spit on me or something like that. All abuse is wrong, but emotional abuse and girl gossip is far worse. It became unbearable. There were slam books that went around school. These were spiral notebooks that students used to "slam" other students. Each student would have pages with their names at the top. Writers would gossip or write horrible things about the person on his or her page. I found a slam book that was left in the gym. I opened it and was reading pages. Then, I found "my page." It was full of words like "lesbo," "dyke," "whore," "don't take a shower during gym because she will stare at you the whole time." I remember reading those sentences and more. I had my mother check me out of school, and I cried for hours. My mother did not know about me being a lesbian or the abuse until that day. I never went back to that school. My mother transferred me to another school in the district. I finished out my junior and senior year at the new school. After high school, I went away to college. I am about to graduate with a degree in education. I am planning to attend graduate school and become a school counselor.

STEPHEN

I came out in high school to a few close friends. One of those friends told someone else, and it eventually got around the school. It was a very small high school in the middle of nowhere. I was picked on all of the time. I was called every name, faggot, fag, sissy, and lots more. I was in two fights, and suspended both times. I was trying to protect myself, but I guess I was just supposed to let someone beat the crap out of me. High school was bad. I was spat on, kicked in the bathroom. It sucked. I skipped school as much as I could without it making me fail. I learned that I could miss up to a certain number of days with excuses, and still make up the work. So, I did. I learned that high school can be a mean place. I am now in a community college doing well. It is a lot different. I am not sure where I will go after, but I think I want to be a history teacher.

BRETT

High school was generally a very uncomfortable place for me; not so much the classroom, but the school bus and entering and exiting school mostly. I was taunted daily by a fellow student on the bus (who, it turns out is gay himself). Kids would be considered *cool* if they called me out or asked me if I was gay. I remember being asked one day in the hall by someone that lived down the road from me (paraphrasing) "I don't mean to offend you or anything, but *are* you gay?" This was in front of several of his friends, and obviously meant to be offensive, not merely curious. I tried to laugh it off as if it were obviously not true, but it obviously wasn't funny to me.

It certainly wasn't that I was flamboyant, or dated guys, or did anything else that would allude to homosexuality. Ok, sure, I blow-dried my hair every day and never left the house without product in my hair. I think the biggest source of speculation was the complete lack of athleticism. Gym class was a place I tried to avoid as much as possible, especially if we were doing something involving catching or throwing a ball (which was about 90% of the time).

Growing up in a (relatively) small New England town, I didn't really know what it meant to be gay, and certainly never had any gay experiences. I knew I found certain guys at school very attractive, but at the same time, didn't think it was an option to act on those feelings. It wasn't until I moved away to college, to a bigger city, that I realized that this isn't completely unacceptable, and started to have relationships with other guys. Before that, I "dated" girls, a term I use loosely, and never dreamed this could be a future lifestyle.

The "dating" consisted of holding hands and the occasional kiss. The thought of going any further was terrifying. I'm not sure if it was truly because I didn't want to, or whether I was just afraid I would do something wrong, or possibly some other reason altogether. If I thought there was a chance that the encounter would lead to something sexual, I would try to avoid it, which after a while, started to infuriate my girlfriend. There were two times I couldn't avoid it, and it was awkward (as maybe it is with most people) but not nearly as terrifying as I had envisioned.

SUZE

My high school experience was not as bad as my gay male friends. Being female, I think that it is a different kind of torture. My male friends were pushed and sometimes fought. But, with me it was more verbal and more emotional. I remember the insults. I think I was called a dyke every day. I was always picked on because of the way I dressed or my hair. The popular girls always called me a man or a boy because I did not wear make-up and because I wore boy jeans. I learned that I had to buy clothes at places where other students did not go. So, I avoided the popular stores so no one would see me in the men's section. So, not only was I a lesbian, but I also did not wear the expensive clothes. I didn't want to give them one more thing to pick on me about. At times, I hated going to school. I did have a group of friends who I chilled with, and they were picked on too for different reasons. High school was just a rough place.

For many non-heterosexual individuals, high school can be a difficult experience. But, the same difficulty exists within in higher education, as well. For John, a professor with whom I spoke, higher education is not always a safe place to express one's true identity. For him, his university climate mirrors the experiences of the high school students above. There is little support for non-heterosexual faculty members on his campus and the language and intolerance towards non-heterosexuality is quite rampant. In fact, he shared stories concerning his coming out process on campus, which did not happen until after he received tenure. Thus, in order to shield himself from intolerance and perhaps protect himself through the tenure process, John remained closeted for seven years.

To further illuminate the reality of some post-secondary experiences, I offer the following story from a current student in the Midwest.

Evan is a sophomore at a fairly large state institution. He self-identifies as a gay male. During his freshman year, he decided to come out in one of his classes. Immediately, he felt ridiculed and judged for being different. He felt as though everyone changed their view of him after his comments. Although his comments aligned with the class discussion that day, he believes his professor even treated him differently. Having said that, according to Evan, his experiences were not the first homophobic experiences on his campus. He retold a story concerning a friend who was physically accosted on campus. It was late one evening and his friend was walking back to his dorm. A group of guys "jumped him and beat the crap out of him." I questioned whether the incident was truly against his friend's sexuality. To which Evan responded, "when they are hitting him and yelling [the F word] it probably means they are doing it because they don't like gays."

Evan's experiences and those of his friend are not atypical for a college community. From a quick Google search, one can locate numerous stories of gays and lesbians being harassed and beaten by others while attending college. For many non-heterosexual identities, there is a fear of coming out or having their sexual identity being discovered by others. In many ways, the fear of not being able to live freely is just as paralyzing as the physical and verbal assaults which others have faced.

Again, it is important to note, I have not chosen to include these individuals' stories to solicit a "victimization" account of homophobia in schools. But rather, I include these stories to provide a framework for educators to truly conceptualize the reality of the effects of homophobia in schools. I postulate that for many educators, recognition of homophobia requires a connection to a "real" student, not simply a list of statistics about school bullying incidents and name calling.

In recognizing the challenges of homophobia in educational settings, I posit that educators must recognize the existence of heteronormativity and specifically a "straight privilege" in schools. By "straight privilege" I mean, a set of benefits or presumptions that heterosexual individuals function within and often take for granted. For example, a heterosexual student can be almost certain that his or her classmates and teachers will be comfortable with his or her sexuality. Also, a heterosexual individual's sexuality is broadly displayed within the school's media, the curricula, and the yearbook, etc. Moreover, heterosexual individuals are rarely accosted because of their sexual orientation. These are all examples of "straight privilege" and how it functions in schools. As with other privileges, "straight privileges" exists because of hegemonic practices within schools that dictate a normalization of sexuality.

Recognizing homophobia and heterosexism in schools is vitally important in unnormalizing education. Educators must realize how "straight privilege" impacts non-heterosexual individuals on a daily basis. They must recognize the broad epidemic of homophobic bullying in schools and universities. Unnormalizing sexuality begins with a recognition of the hegemonic practices that exists within schooling, and in order to do that, one must acknowledge the problem of homophobia.

NOTES

1. All names are pseudonyms to protect individual identities.
2. Jason's story and the ones that follow are referenced from *Making Safe Places Unsafe: A Discussion of Homophobia With Teachers.*

CHAPTER 2

(UN)MASKING OUR TRUE TOLERANCE

I think it is all part of the publicity of schools. Tolerance is a big thing in society. So schools compete with each other and say, "we are tolerant and supportive." In my school, they do that, but there is still so much prejudice for anyone who is different. It becomes a publicity competition for school districts. We are a better district than they are.

—Beth

It is easy to say "I value you. You are part of my community." It is hard to show someone how valuable he or she is to you and your community. That is what we need to do in higher education. We need to do a better job of showing.

—Tara

Anti-oppressive education examines and explores how schools become places where "racism, sexism, and other 'isms' find life" (Center for Anti-Oppressive Education, 2010). According to the Center for Anti-Oppressive Education (2012), "'oppression' refers to a social dynamic in which certain ways of being in this world—including certain ways of identifying or being identified—are normalized or privileged while other ways are disadvantaged or marginalized." Thus, oppressive education involves the marginalization of individuals through the process of social normalization. Specifically, the "marginalized" groups of individuals in schools have rejected the notions of "accepted" normal behaviors and identities; therefore, those groups are labeled as the "others" in the school community. In doing so, the labeling constructs an oppressive educational environment, through which intolerance of differences cultivates.

In order to truly unnormalize education, we must begin examining the role of tolerance in our schooling process and how the level influences the lives of non-heterosexual identities. Specifically, tolerance plays a tremendous role in creating supportive schools. In broad terms and relating to schooling, I define tolerance as a permissive attitude of accepting others views, beliefs, and identities, and in doing so removing the binary structures that exists in the constructions of "otherness." In such a capacity, educational environments should provide tolerant places where students feel validated; so that they can engage in the learning process. In order to be truly tolerant, educators must recognize and acknowledge the idea that there should be no one dominant culture within school communities. In doing so, educators can create a school that values the concepts of respect for all individuals, acceptance of differences among cultures, and understanding other cultures (Baptiste, 1979). However, the tolerance must be authentic.

Colleary and Kluth (2002) define authentic tolerance as places where there is a genuine mutual respect for differences among individuals. According to multiculturalism, tolerance is important in schools because it causes individuals to begin to move toward a mutual respect for all students (Banks, 2007). Thus, tolerance is just a step toward acceptance. Further, an authentic tolerance should protect all students from harassment, including harassment that is a result of differences in sexual identity (Jones, 2011c). According to GLSEN (2008), creating tolerant schools and classrooms is a vital aspect in addressing homophobia.

Although authentic tolerance is vital, it does not always exist within educational environments. Many schools members project tolerant attitudes toward others; however, their tolerance is unauthentic. An unauthentic tolerance is one where a school member or community outwardly proclaims an acceptance of difference but secretly creates intolerant spaces for non-heterosexual individuals.

In a recent study I conducted with a group of teachers, the findings indicate a false tolerance exists in these participants' classrooms and schools. Participants shared the belief that a false sense of tolerance is projected by their districts to their communities. For example, a teacher identifies a degree of hypocrisy within her school district. She states, "People may not like homosexuals, but we still pride ourselves as being an open school and as soon as someone comes out, it's like the red state blue state thing. We pride ourselves on this tolerance and when it comes right down to it, we don't have an authentic tolerance." In a conversation with Matt, a high school English teacher, he argues, "It's funny how we can pretend that everything is okay. We say we can be open and accepting, but it's far from the truth. I was afraid to come out because I knew what would happen. I see it all the time. The bad thing is it is just as bad among the faculty as it is with the students."

These teachers' beliefs about their school communities are similar to Michelle's beliefs about her school. Michelle believes that her school is incredibly intolerant. In her school, there is a gay and lesbian student club, but a majority of the school population makes negative comments about the club, and the club does not receive publication space in the school newspaper or yearbook. She has even heard faculty and staff make negative comments about the "gay kid club." Further, she indicates that her school leaders and fellow faculty members all want the outside community to believe that their school is progressive and tolerant of difference. Yet, she does not believe her school is a tolerant environment.

In these examples, these educators discuss their views about the level of tolerance within their schools. Specifically, one teacher believes the tolerance in her school is not authentic. In fact, she believes when individuals come out, the school becomes divided much like a political debate concerning non-heterosexuality. Further, Matt was afraid to come out because he believed that his building was only pretending to be open and accepting of different sexualities. Because of this false tolerance, Matt was forced to remain closeted and to project a heterosexual identity to his school community. It is also important that Matt argues that this intolerance is equally shared among the faculty and students.

Michelle's statement also suggests a false tolerance and a level of hypocrisy. By allowing students to comment negatively on the gay and lesbian club, the school supports a false tolerance. For Michelle, this hypocrisy influences the ways the school population treats non-heterosexual students. As with the others, Michelle believes her school district wants the community to believe that it is progressive and tolerant; however, she sees no evidence to support the school's claim. Michelle also makes the statement, "it's a line that we are giving." This statement suggests that her school does not have an authentic tolerance toward gay and lesbian students. In addition to these teachers' beliefs about tolerance, Kirk, another teacher with whom I was working made the following statement:

> My school tells everyone that we are tolerant because we have the suburban-urban program. They believe that having that program creates tolerance, but there is still prejudices there. It's the same for gay and lesbian kids. We say we have had a GSA for 11 years, but we don't invest in the club. We don't engage in teaching students about difference. It's a club that fills a space in the school community. Yeah, we have a GSA, but no activities around the lives of GLBT students.

Kirk implies a level of false tolerance in the ways the school address racial identity and sexual identity. His statements suggest that his school wants everyone to believe that it is tolerant and supportive of non-heterosexual students, but there are no actions to support that claim. In a number of ways, tolerance has become the buzzword for many educational environments. In such a capacity, being a tolerant school has become an aspect of the publicity of schools (Jones, 2010).

As with K–12 schools, I postulate the college campus also maintains a sense of a false tolerance. In a recent study, I surveyed public and private schools in the Commonwealth of Virginia. The anonymous surveys were sent electronically to every public and non-religiously affiliated private school in the commonwealth. Approximately 1,500 faculty, staff, and students answered the survey. To me, the results were quite shocking. Forty percent of the respondents stated that they have heard homophobic slurs being made on their campus, 15% of which were made by faculty or staff members. When asked an open-ended question about their beliefs concerning their college climate, many respondents responded with statements such as, "we have problems with tolerance here, but no one addresses it," or "it is not safe here for GLBTQ students." A number of respondents specifically mentioned incidents on their own campuses. For example, several respondents discussed an incident with one student who had recently had homophobic slurs scratched into his car. The student had the repairs made, but the same words were inscribed again into the new paint job. These participants also discussed how the appropriate actions were not conducted to address this challenge. I assume the participants who recounted this story were all from the same university because I did not ask for participants to list their college name. It should be noted, all of these schools publicly embrace an adherence to diversity and tolerance.

In further discussing the notions of tolerance on the college campus, one professor commented about his school's false tolerance during a conversation with me. He stated, "Our school has major problems with homophobia and other types of hatred. We all know it is there and how horrible it is. But, the administration does not want to address it. We have a restaurant on campus that donates large sums of money to hate groups of all sorts. Nothing has been done to remove the restaurant from our campus. Yet, if you talk to administration and read our website, you would think we were incredibly tolerant. We want everyone to believe that we value diversity. But, I work here. I have had countless conversations with colleagues. It simply is not true."

In these school communities, I postulate there is a false tolerance within these educational environments. Although these schools project tolerant attitudes to their communities, these participants believe this projected belief is not the reality in their individual schools. In such a capacity, their unauthentic tolerance is creating a school that participates in a covert het-erocentricity, which is a projection of a tolerant atmosphere, but secretly continuing to marginalize non-heterosexual identities. Covert hetero-centricity exists in institutions and continues to be a system of prejudice that marginalizes individuals, and create oppressive educational environ-ments. It provides schools with the ability to pretend to be tolerant but to still maintain and support the social normative ideologies that surround beliefs concerning sexual identity. Covert heterocentricity dictates and perpetuates unsafe environments for non-heterosexual students. In doing so, these educational environments become places where homophobia thrives, because of a covert heterocentricity. Thus, covert heterocentricity allows school communities to engage in a regulatory practice that governs the notions surrounding tolerance of sexual identity within these school communities. It is the regulation of the dominant culture that dictates the level of tolerance within the communities.

This is problematic because such school environments continue to per-petuate homophobia, but also such behaviors teach students and other school members that such covert behaviors are acceptable within the edu-cational environment. Therefore, I posit that unmasking our true tolerance towards non-heterosexual identities is an imperative step in the process of unnormalizing education. In doing so, we must understand an authentic tolerance, and how an authentic tolerance impacts the school environment.

In understanding and attaining an authentic tolerance, we must rec-ognize the level of hypocrisy that exists in educational environments concerning issues surrounding non-heterosexual individuals. As discussed above, Matt was afraid to come out because he believed that his building was only pretending to be open and accepting of different sexualities. Because of the school community's false tolerance, he was forced to remain closeted and to project a heterosexual identity to his school community and peers. The teacher argued that this intolerance toward different sexual identities is equally shared among the faculty and students (Jones, 2010).

The notion of a false tolerance indicates a need for schools to examine how educators and administrators are indeed addressing issues surround-ing diversity and inclusion in their schools, classrooms, and on their campuses. I posit that unmasking our true tolerance allows us the ability to recognize our own biases and how those biases engender intolerant schools and classrooms, which in turn, helps create anti-oppressive educa-tional settings.

The recognition of a need to engage in an authentic tolerance allows educators to begin to conceptualize the idea and necessity of a "profes-sional tolerance." A professional tolerance is one that is characterized by an ability to separate one's personal beliefs from the professional purposes and objectives. Ethically, it is every educator's responsibility to create safe environments for all students (Jones, 2010). To that end, teachers and administrators must create atmospheres where students are not afraid to come to class and where students can receive an appropriate education without a fear of being bullied or harassed. Although, a teacher may have strong socialized beliefs against non-heterosexual identities, those beliefs should not be imposed into the classroom setting or on students at any level of education. Engaging in a professional tolerance commences the beginning process of unnormalizing education because it allows educators to separate their personal socialized views of different sexualities from the educational environment.

In exploring the notions of tolerance, it is necessary to briefly recount a recent experience I had while presenting on creating tolerant and safe college environments. After discussing my beliefs about tolerance in the university and a recent research study that I have conducted, an individual made the following statement, "I do not agree with your premise. As a gay male at this university, I do not want people to simply be tolerant of me and my lifestyle. In fact, I do not want to be tolerated. Rather, I want to be accepted, to be loved and to be welcomed." The gentleman continued to propose tolerance was equitable to homophobia and hatred. The only difference being tolerance is guised as being an acceptable form of such hatred.

Although I acknowledge his desire to be accepted, and I recognize his animosity towards tolerance, as with many marginalized groups, this gentleman was not fully conceptualizing the role tolerance plays within our communities, nor was he willing to recognize the process of becoming a more accepting and affirming community. In order to truly unnormalize education, it is imperative to understand the reality of homophobia and how homophobia functions within our society and within individuals. The reality is no one is able to make another human "love and welcome" him into his or her community. We live in a world that is incredibly situated with social norms that are embedded within solidified hegemonic structures. Each of those hegemonic structures exists because of the imbalance of power within our society. To assume that one can simply demand another individual to love, to affirm and to welcome him, refuses to conceptualize the very underpinnings of social normative ideologies and how those ideologies control entire communities. Thus, in order to create change in communities, we must recognize the process of change. Specifically, I postulate combating homophobia within schools, universities and the broader society entails engaging individuals in a personal reflective journey.

A personal reflective journey is vitally important in creating safe and tolerant schools. Later, in this text, I discuss the personal journey; however, I do believe it is important to discuss the four stages of creating safe schools: acknowledgment, authentic tolerance, acceptance and affirmation.

Acknowledgment involves the recognition of the homophobia within one's community. The acknowledgment can range from acknowledging a systemic problem with homophobia or it can be confined to a personal level of one acknowledging his or her own homophobia. Acknowledgment is the first step in one's personal journey. He or she must recognize the problem of homophobia and how homophobic actions are problematic. Secondly, in order to create a safe educational environment for non-heterosexual individuals, one must maintain an authentic tolerance. This chapter was devoted to the importance of an authentic tolerance. Thirdly, a community and individuals must reach a level of acceptance for non-heterosexual individuals. Acceptance involves a genuine respect for non-heterosexual identities and proposes a belief in the ability to cohabitate with GLBTQ individuals. The final step in creating a safe environment for non-heterosexual individuals involves the affirmation of GLBTQ individuals' lives and identities. Affirmation involves embracing the "other" that exists within the community. In fact, affirmation is the stage that deconstructs the very binary opposition that controls the ideology of otherness. Affirmation dismantles the necessity to continue to function within the normalized ideologies of sexual identity. In order to unnormalize education, our communities must engage in all four steps of the process.

Because of this process, it is imperative to conceptualize the process of creating an affirming community. The young man who wanted "to be loved and affirmed" does not recognize the individual and community process necessary to achieve affirmation. It is necessary to first develop an authentic tolerance towards difference and develop acceptance and affirmation.

CHAPTER 3

(UN)RAVELING MASCULINITIES AND HEGEMONY

It won't jive with what a male athlete is supposed to be.

—Jennifer Ball, PhD

Several months ago, I was discussing with a group of practicing teachers and pre-service teachers the role gender identity plays in the lives of our community. We discussed the roles and genders society place upon each member of the community. In our discussions, I began discussing the book, *My Princess Boy,* and was seeking to conceptualize how this group of educators felt about the book. It was my hope to provide the group with a different perspective of how forced gender roles impact everyone in our community: parents, students, and teachers. To my surprise, few of the educators were aware of the book.

For those who are unfamiliar with the book, I borrow the synopsis from the cover:

> *My Princess Boy* is a nonfiction picture book about acceptance. I wrote the story to give children and adults a tool to talk about unconditional friendship. When I feared my young son would be teased or bullied for wearing a dress to school. I spoke with his preschool teacher. She shared my fears with others, and a plan was put in place to support him and others who express themselves differently. In light of the many unthinkable outcomes of bully-

(Un)normalizing Education:
Addressing Homophobia in Higher Education and K–12 Schools, pp. 19–25
Copyright © 2014 by Information Age Publishing

ing, discussion about acceptance can help get our world back to the basics—compassion. How can we be compassionate with one another? Compassion takes effort. It takes focus. It takes commitment. We need practice. And more practice. And practice again. We are an ecosystem. Our compassion for one another and the broader world is dependent upon one another. And when we interconnect, we celebrate the unique person within us all. (Kilodavis, 2011)

After reading the book to the group, the group had mixed feelings concerning using the text in an elementary classroom and the impact the book may have on the views of the community, especially parents. Many believed the book taught a valuable lesson; however, they also believed the book would be a catalyst for parental complaints. As we reflected on the possible causes of parental complaints, one major theme emerged, perceptions.

As human beings, we make judgments on others because of our perceptions about those individuals. We perceive someone's intelligence based on his or her job. We perceive someone's wealth by his or her materials. Perceptions of others and our world are pivotal to our constructed worldviews. As such, perceptions play a tremendous role in our understandings of others and sexual identities. As human beings, perceptions are a part of all our lives, whether they are correct or incorrect. Many perceptions are also predicated on hegemony and hegemonic practices. Hegemony exists within schools and engenders what behaviors are acceptable based upon normative social constructions.

Therefore, hegemony permits educational environments to allow non-heterosexual identities to exist but not completely affirm them. One form of hegemony that continues to control perceptions within universities and school is hegemonic masculinity.

For the purpose of this discussion, I define hegemonic masculinity as a belief or ideology that males should be able to control others, specifically perceived weaker males. Additionally, hegemonic masculinity rejects any behavior or person who threatens the ideals of what it means to be a masculine male. Hegemonic masculinity is a pervasive ideology that permeates schools, and in doing so allows homophobia to be premised on an accepted masculinity. I define an accepted masculinity as one where biological males displayed to their communities appropriate masculine attributes. As with other notions of sexuality, these masculine attributes are socialized constructions of what a community defines as normal masculine characteristics. Thus, an appropriate socialized male behavior with masculine attributes guarantees the dominant position of some men in educational settings. To that end, hegemonic masculinity insists that men must reach the ideal level of masculinity to be accepted within the school community, in turn, continuing the patriarchal dominance that exists within society and schools (Jones, 2010).

Because of an accepted masculinity in schools, I postulate that a majority of homophobic acts are directed toward individuals who do not display the appropriate masculine attributes to their communities. Thus, homophobia is not about an innate sexual identity, but rather homophobia is about a perceived sexuality identity. Homophobia is about a perception of one's sexual identity that is predicated on the individual's level of masculinity. Therefore, a majority of homophobic acts are directed toward effeminate males (Jones, 2010). By effeminate males, I mean biological males who do not conform to socially constructed masculine attributes. I believe this is a tremendous distinction that must be recognized in order to begin truly destroying heteronormativity and homophobia.

In a recent interview, educators constantly defined and discussed homophobic actions directed toward non-masculine identities or effeminate males. Most of the educators believe that non-masculine males attract a large amount of homophobia within their school communities. For example, one teacher discussed how her student wore a "big purple boa to class … and everyone picked on this kid" (Jones, 2010, p. 37). She continues to discuss how the student received verbal and physical harassment. She attributed this harassment to his display of feminine characteristics. Other teachers in the interview also recognized how their communities treated individuals who do not adhere to the constructed normalized definitions of masculinity.

In the same interview, a veteran high school teacher, describes how a socially appropriate level of masculinity shielded one student from being a target of homophobic bullying. It was her belief that because the student played on the high school's lacrosse team and projected a very masculine persona, he was not ridiculed because of his sexuality (Jones, 2010). For this student, his displays of an appropriate masculinity, ones that his school community deemed as appropriate, protected him from harassment.

Further, one teacher, in a middle school, witnessed a morning announcement video created by students for the school. Typically, the morning announcement video in her school models a morning news show. On one day, the morning announcements portrayed a male student giving the weather forecast. In the video, the student "pretended to be the weather fairy with a lisp" (Jones, 2010). This depiction becomes an interpretation of the student's learned behavior of what masculine and non-masculine traits, by extension what heterosexual and non-heterosexual traits are; all of which are constructed within binary oppositions. By "pretending" to have this attribute, the student "acts" like a gay male. His depiction constructs his beliefs about sexual identity.

In addition to this depiction, Matt discussed how his class was winding down and a group of students began laughing. One male student stood, dropped his wrists (in a stereotypical gay manner), and walked down the aisle shaking his hips back and forth saying 'look at me, I am a little faggot' (Jones, 2011) According to Matt, there was a self-identified gay student who is out and a little flamboyant in the class. In his discussion, Matt identifies the actions of the male student as homophobic.

Moreover, in his reflective journal, Brian writes, "I saw a student in class walk over to another student that I assume is gay. He has not told me that he is a gay. But, I think he is. The first kid drops his wrist and speaks in a very high pitched voice to the kid sitting down. That's my chair. Your chair is in the back by your boyfriend. He then laughed at the gay student and then started pushing him out of the chair." As with the other teachers, Brian also identified this action as an example of homophobia.

Another example of how hegemonic masculinity pervades the schooling process is how Sue describes a high school senior making a homophobic remark. Sue had asked one of her students to work with an openly self-identified gay student. The heterosexual student stood and removed his John Deere hat. He looked at the teacher and stated, "I'm not working with that fucking [F word]." According to the Sue, the heterosexual male was "acting out his homophobia" and his distaste for homosexuality in front of the teacher and the class. Sue's example illustrates how homophobia becomes a way for individuals to reinforce socially constructed and per-ceived sexual identities. The heterosexual male stood (an act of power and dominance), removed his hat, and spoke. By these actions, the heterosexual male was displaying his learned and perceived masculine heterosexual identity in front of the teacher and the class (Leitch et al., 2001). In doing so, the student was reinforcing for the teacher and his classmates his learned depiction of what a "real man" acts likes and rejects any anti-nor-mal non-masculine identity roles. Further, the student was wearing a John Deere hat; in doing so, his hat becomes part of his masculinity and sexu-ality. In western culture, John Deere is an archetype of masculinity. John Deere is a company known in the United States for agricultural machinery and is culturally connected to masculinity. Thus, the hat that the student is wearing reinforces his own perceived masculinity and sexuality as a display for his community.

In all of these examples, there is a performance of masculinity which is a result of the hegemonic masculinity that exists within these schools. In such a capacity, males within society must display appropriate dominant attributes to be accepted and not be labeled as deviants, as a result of patriarchal authority. For example, the male student who depicted the "weather fairy with a lisp" was asserting his masculinity by performing in a manner that was derogatory of non-masculine identities. The male who dropped his wrists and performed in front of his classmates was also asserting his masculinity by engaging in homosexual stereotypes. He also forcefully attempted to push the other student out of the chair, by doing so, attempting to prove his dominance over the perceived weaker student. Likewise, the student in the John Deere hat asserted his dominance over the self-identified non-heterosexual student to continue to maintain his perceived dominant power over others within his school community. Thus, all of these males engaged in performances that reinforced their own perceived masculine identities to their community.

In these school communities, hegemonic masculinity plays a tremendous role in the ways that the students exert their own power over others who are perceived to be weaker. To add to this, these males were also creating dramatic performances that illustrate their distaste for non-heterosexuality. In these examples, the students are "acting out their homophobia" in order to be perceived by their classmates as straight masculine males (Nowlan, 2008). Thus, these incidents do not only reinforce hegemonic masculinity, but they also reveal how heteronormativity is perpetuated within schools. Specifically, heteronormativity is reproduced in these schools through the dramatic performances of a heterosexuality identity (Nowlan, 2008).

In the above examples, these participants discussed specific actions that took place within their school buildings, actions that are manifestations of prejudices towards non-heterosexual identities.

In these school communities, these educators have constructed an acceptable definition of what it means to be masculine and such masculinity is the deciding factor for determining who receives harassment. This level of masculinity is premised on the notions of a hegemonic masculinity. In these communities, individuals have learned through socialization in their communities appropriate masculine characteristics. Thus, if a boy wears a boa to class, he becomes marginalized and harassed because he is perceived as rejecting the community's constructed categories of femininity and masculinity. Moreover, in this community's normative constructions of identity, the boy with the boa is the antithesis of a masculine male who should have the power to subordinate others. Therefore, those males who are less masculine in these participants' schools are the ones who defy the rules of hegemony, thus becoming the targets of homophobia.

Further, the harassment of the students becomes a way for this society to perpetuate heteronormativity and appropriate gender roles. In doing so, the members of this community are equating sexuality with a perceived gender. These school communities have determined that because this student is effeminate he must be gay. Thereby, these school communities have based sexual orientation on a displayed/perceived gender. Specifically, effeminate males receive harassment because their displays of gender do not adhere to the normative scripts of gender identity for their community. Therefore, this harassment is predicated on a socially perceived gender identity, not necessarily a sexual orientation, all of which are controlled by hegemonic masculinity.

Hegemonic masculinity within schools is also replicated through the acceptance of certain romantic behaviors. Specifically, I postulate the existence of a romantic affection among same-sex couples that is accepted and at times encouraged by the school population. In a recent study, a teacher discussed same sex affection in her school, "You never see any 'boy on boy' affection, but 'girl on girl' affection happens all the time in the hallways." For this teacher, "girl on girl" sexuality was more accepted within her school. In fact, she noted few homophobic remarks directed toward perceived lesbian couples: "The vast majority of homophobia is directed toward boy-on-boy relationships" (Jones, 2014).

Another teacher also discussed this notion of "girl-on-girl" versus "boy-on-boy" homophobia: "male homosexuality is incredibly taboo in my school. But, I have noticed that students and faculty seem to be more tolerant of lesbianism."

According to the findings in this study, lesbian affection is more accepted within these teachers' high schools than gay male affection. The teachers in the study noticed differences between the ways individuals in the schools react to male non-heterosexual affection and lesbian affection. Male non-heterosexual affection in these participants' schools is more taboo because socially constructed concepts of appropriate male behavior are more defined within society. Specifically, socially constructed appropriate male behavior denies two males showing romantic affection.

The acceptance of lesbian affection over gay male affection in schools illuminates the reality of hegemonic masculinity within schools. Specifically, alternatives are allowed but not completely accepted within these schools because of the notions of hegemonic masculinity. Specifically, hegemonic masculinity proposes a culturally accepted male behavior which males must attain. This male behavior guarantees the dominant position of some men over others. Hegemonic masculinity posits that men must reach the ideal level of masculinity to be accepted within the community, in turn, continuing the patriarchal dominance that exists within society. Thus, in these participants' schools there is a sense of acceptance of lesbian affection because such affection does not disrupt the hegemonic masculinity that exists within these schools and by extension the broader community. Conversely, the acceptance of gay male affections contradicts the rules of becoming a dominant male in society. These schools reject male non-heterosexual affection because it threatens the perpetuation of an ideal male behavior. In order to unnormalize education, educators, at all levels, must acknowledge how hegemonic masculinity functions within educational settings. Hegemonic masculinity controls the ways through which individuals construct knowledge about homophobia in their schools and their communities. Indeed, it is one of the foundational aspects of socialized normative beliefs against non-heterosexual identities.

Hegemonic masculinity plays a tremendous role within the schooling process. In such a capacity, it is important to conceptualize the commencement point of hegemonic masculinity. Specifically, children learn a very young age what it means to be male and female. According to Leitch et al. (2001), "The little boy learns that his crying is not masculine; he must grow into his masculinity by imitating the behavior designated as 'male' to the point that such behavior becomes 'second nature'" (p. 2486). The same process applies to biologically female children. Each child learns from others of the same gender appropriate gender behaviors and inappropriate gender behaviors. It is through this process, children display their socially normative and appropriate gender and sexual identity to their communities. All of this happens because of hegemonic practices. Because a patriarchal society values accepted masculine behaviors, hegemonic masculinity controls the normative processes for genders within society, especially biological male genders.

Thus, in order to create safe schools for non-heterosexual identities, the process of schooling must dismantle the normalizing process of what it means to be a biological male and biological female within society. In doing so, schools must break free from the binary oppositions that dictate appropriate gender roles for the community, an important aspect of the process of unnormalizing education.

CHAPTER 4

(UN)DOING THE HIERARCHY OF HATE LANGUAGE

Why isn't someone saying something about kids being called these names.

—Leslie Daniel, PhD

Recently, while watching a national news station, I viewed a leading story about a celebrity who was being publicly humiliated for his or her use of racist language. Although the celebrity publicly apologized for his or her language choices, the celebrity was quickly losing large commercial endorsements, and it appears the celebrity may lose millions of dollars because of his or her racist language. In essence, it appears his or her career may be ending. Within the same week, another celebrity used a homophobic slur. To my knowledge, this celebrity has not apologized for his or her language choices, nor has he or she been publicly reprimanded for the use of the homophobic language. Although both language choices were inappropriate and hateful to a specific marginalized group, the broader society has leveraged a stronger reprimand on the use of the racist language, than the use of the homophobic language.

In an interview which I conducted with a group of educators, one teacher brought up the idea of racism and how racial slurs are treated much differently than homophobic slurs in her school building. One teacher, whom I will call Steve, agreed with her and stated, "The other day in my school a

---

(Un)normalizing Education:
Addressing Homophobia in Higher Education and K–12 Schools, pp. 27–30

student called another student 'the n word.' The other student punched the kid. The student who used the racist language was suspended, while nothing happened to the student who became violent."

After Steve told his story, the group of teachers all began a lively conversation involving their own thoughts about how their school administrators addressed racial language incidents in schools differently than homophobic language incidents. For this group of teachers, their experiences in schools suggested that racist slurs did indeed receive harsher reprimands than other forms of other hate language, especially homophobic hate language.

In the same discussion, another teacher was discussing a visit he made to another school in his district. As he walked into the main hallway, he heard repetitive homophobic slurs. There were teachers in the hallways, yet no one addressed the students using the language. He decided to count the number of times that he heard the word. His calculated number was around 27 times. As he was recounting his story to us in the professional development, he stated, "If that had been the N word, then someone would have said that there is a toxic racism in this building, but nothing was done about the homophobic slurs." In fact, teachers in the hallways did not even acknowledge the use of the homophobic words.

Unfortunately, his claim was probably true. Our schools and society have become places where a hierarchy of hate language has been constructed, and each day that hierarchy is supported through the daily actions of teachers and administrators. By this I mean, schools have created a systemic problem with their treatment of hate language. Specifically, the N word is treated in a manner that acknowledges the damaging aspects of racist language; conversely, the F word is simply a "popular culture" phrase that does not receive the necessary attention from school leaders and personnel. In doing so, I postulate that schools have created a hierarchy of hate language. Specifically, the N word is something that is not tolerated in most school environments, and when used, the person is reprimanded appropriately. In fact, in some school communities, the word is incredibly taboo to repeat. Conversely, the F word, is acceptable to verbalize and repeat because that word is not viewed as a "negative word," and because of the socialized beliefs about non-heterosexual identities. In doing so, this hierarchy in language dictates how we address homophobia and homophobic slurs in our school communities.

This is problematic because hierarchies have power. They provide us with the ability to structure our understandings of our world in a way that excludes others and reinforces the notions of power that exists in our communities. In doing so, the power structure reinforces the belief systems of the community. Specifically, I argue the hierarchy of hate language that exists within schools, and by extension, in society continues to perpetuate a mentality of complacency. If individuals and communities do not believe that all hate language, regardless of the marginalized population, should be addressed equally, discrimination and prejudice will also be treated within the same hierarchical structure. In doing so, homophobic language will continue to be accepted and receive less attention than racist language, although both types of language are detrimental to the entire community. The impact of placing hate language within a hierarchy is quite troublesome, and educational communities must devise methods to dismantle the hierarchy, which is not an easy task.

To further discuss the difficult ability to break free from the hierarchy of language, I would like to discuss how incredibly entwined the hierarchy of language is in our lives. I argue that the teachers who participated in the professional development discussed above were aware of the damaging effects of homophobia and homophobic slurs in schools. In fact, some of the teachers were faculty advisors for their school's Gay Straight Alliance (GSA). Yet, even their own language choices were dictated to some degree by the hierarchy of language.

For example, during the professional development, the topic of racism emerged in our discussions. I was amazed to hear each teacher use the phrase, "the n word." No one said the actual racial slur. In contrast, even after discussing homophobic language and deciding what language was distinctly homophobic, this group of teachers continued to use the homophobic language, but continued to say "the n word," no one ever said "the f word," rather the teachers used the actual homophobic slur.

As a researcher and a teacher educator, I began contemplating how this group of teachers treated the use of hate language in the professional development. Although these teachers had dedicated themselves to creating safe places for non-heterosexual identities and discussed how important it is to address all hate language equally, their own treatment and use of hate language suggests the true influence of this hierarchy of language on the discussions revolving around homophobia and hate. On some level, they felt comfortable saying homophobic slurs but did not feel comfortable saying racist slurs (Jones, 2010).

In addition to the professional development with the teachers above, I decided to examine the phenomenon (in an informal manner) in my courses at the university. In all of my courses (both graduate and undergraduate) there is a necessary place to discuss marginalized students and how schools deal with issues surrounding diversity. During one of our class discussions, I asked the students to discuss their experiences with hate language. I followed up this query with other appropriate questions. Most of the students discussed how the N word was addressed quite differently than the F word, if the F word was addressed as all. Some students shared their experiences with faculty and staff using the homophobic language, but rarely heard those same individuals using racist language. In my "informal" analysis, the same results emerged as the ones from my formal professional development with the teachers. Those results support the idea of a hierarchy of hate language that exists in our schools. For these groups of teachers, it was acceptable to use homophobic language but it was unacceptable to use racist language.

As a former English teacher and currently a professor in a teacher education department, this troubles me greatly. Further, considering the recent deaths of a number of gay students across our country, this placement of hate language into hierarchies is even more worrisome. I wonder why schools have become places where two types of hate language can be treated in such vastly different ways—one is frowned upon and punished immediately while the other is ignored and even used by teachers themselves. Although, it is important to note, I am not suggesting these teachers were homophobic; rather, I am reiterating the power and function of a constructed hierarchy of hate language and how pervasively the hierarchy has permeated our society.

I believe all of the teachers discussed above did not realize the extent to which the hierarchy of language was impacting their own lives, their own classrooms and their own language choices. There is power in social constructions of hierarchies. Social hierarchies have existed in schools for decades. However, the challenge arises when we do not recognize how those hierarchies are impacting our own lives and our own classrooms. I posit that it is imperative for all school personnel to realize the impact of placing hate language into hierarchies. Functioning within a hierarchy of hate language may not matter to some, but it does matter to the non-heterosexual student who happens to be in class.

Moreover, in order to address the challenges of homophobia, we must recognize how homophobia is perpetuated in our schools through the use of language. We must realize that the language that we use does have an impact on the atmosphere in our schools and classrooms, whether that is the phrase "that's so gay" or "the F word." By continuing to allow the hierarchy of hate language to exist in schools, school personnel are reinforcing heteronormativity and homophobia. Specifically, by not addressing all hate language equally and allowing words to be said without reprimand, educators are nonverbally sanctioning the use of homophobic language. In doing so, they are creating school spaces that are not safe for non-heterosexual students.

I further discuss the power of language and the hierarchy of hate language in the next chapter, "(Un)contextualizing Language and Behaviors" because the hierarchy of language is also connected to how society constructs contextual oppositions to conceptualize hate language.

CHAPTER 5

(UN)CONTEXTUALIZING LANGUAGE AND BEHAVIORS

Having a sense that the word can be harmful or hateful to another human being is a connection that has to consciously be made ... having them be responsible for their language is important.

—Allyson S. Linn

In order to truly (un)normalize education and create safe places for non-heterosexual individuals, we must begin conceptualizing how language and behaviors dictate our understandings and identifications of homophobia and homophobic bullying. Thus, I argue that we must break free from the notions of contextual oppositions.

Contextual oppositions are the binary oppositions that individuals construct in order to conceptualize and define homophobia and perhaps other forms of discriminatory practices. It is the process of placing words/actions into binary oppositional relationships through the use of contextual understandings. In order to fully understand how contextual oppositions function within our society, I would like to offer a non-sexuality related example. Several months ago, I was having dinner in Philadelphia with several friends. As we were sitting in the restaurant, an African American male walked over to a nearby table and stated, "What's up N. (He used the racist slur)." From my vantage point, I was able to view everyone involved

(Un)normalizing Education:
Addressing Homophobia in Higher Education and K–12 Schools, pp. 31–36
Copyright © 2014 by Information Age Publishing

in the conversation. My friend sitting opposite to me, with her back to the individuals, only heard the statement. She was appalled. She quickly turned around to view the exchange. When she noticed that the conversation was between two African American males, she returned to her previous placement and continued eating. It was evident that her anger had subsided, and I inquired why she was no longer upset. She responded, "It is different in that situation" (Jones, 2012, p. 8).

Before discussing contextual oppositions in greater depth, it is beneficial to briefly examine the notions of reclaiming language. In that moment, my friend was accepting the attributes of a philosophical belief, reclaiming language. According to Godrej (2003):

> We reclaim terms, words, specific phrases, so that we refashion their meaning to correspond to our particular goals, we rescue or salvage them from their earlier, often derogatory, meanings, we repossess them so that we make them our own, so that their meanings have the authority of our ownership behind them ... reclamation is usually a tool for disarming the power of a dominant group to control one's own and others' views of oneself ... the larger target of the reclamation project is the self-understanding of individuals through a reshaping of a relationship between language and power. (p. 2)

Therefore, reclaiming language involves individuals in marginalized communities who are attempting to reclaim language for their own usage. In simple terms, reclaiming language involves morphing a pejorative term into an acceptable term to be used within a community. The process involves using language that traditionally was used by the dominant culture to oppress or violate marginalized individuals. Proponents of reclaiming language argue that hate language which was once an insult thwarted upon marginalized individuals can be resituated with new positive meanings that are accepted within those same communities that once the words were used against. However, I question whether the acceptance of language within a community is enough to actually remove the historical hatred that was once associated with the language. In fact, I postulate that outside of marginalized communities, the language rarely undergoes the desired change. Thus, no matter how many community members use language in a positive way, the language still maintains the traditional hatred undertones of the original definition.

This is an important discussion to consider because the act of reclaiming language actually hinders the process of unnormalizing education. Reclaiming language does not consider the notions of an entire community. Rather, the focus of reclaiming language is on the sub-culture or the non-dominant culture and its use of language and how the specific community has morphed the hate language into a positive term. For example, if one argues that non-heterosexual identities can use the F word within their own communities, but the broader community is not allowed to use the same word because they lack a membership in non-heterosexual community, does this situation now perpetuate a sense of privilege, dominance, and otherness? Although, it may seem that the "lesser group" is now in control of the hate language and has re-appropriated its meaning, the dominant group is still the one in power and the hate language still has a traditional meaning to the group in power. In simple terms, it is akin to saying to the dominant group, "the word does not mean that anymore, so it does not hurt me. And, to prove it does not hurt, I can use it myself and call myself and my friends the word." As this is being done, the dominant group still embraces the traditional meaning of the word and still maintains a sense of prejudice and hatred each time the word is used.

Moreover, it is necessary to also consider the role of a community in the process of schooling. The process of schooling involves an entire community. As such, equity and tolerance should be a product of a school community. Thus, it matters how the school community behaves toward others, regardless of marginalization. In such a capacity, language choices matter in the context of schooling. Further, reclaiming language initially focuses on marginalized cultures within a broader community. Therefore, I posit reclaiming language may actually perpetuate a dominant and non-dominant binary opposition because it is premised upon the notions of power relations, language, and communities. As such, it does not unite a school community.

Because of the reality of reclaiming language, I postulate schools must reconceptualize how individuals construct meaning concerning language use and behaviors. Specifically, the experience with my friend in Philadelphia revealed how contextual oppositions dictated her understanding, her identifying, and her acceptance of racist language. For her, it was an appropriate use of racist language; she had contextualized the use of racist language. At first, she was upset about hearing the word because of an assumption of the context in which it was spoken. After realizing the context, she was willing to accept the use of the word. In that moment for her, the N word was not a racist slur and in that moment, the reclamation of language was accepted and visual. In doing so, she had contextualized the use of hate language into a structure which I call "contextual oppositions." The traditional meaning of the word did not change, but by contextualizing the word, she ascribed a non-racist definition to the word. I argue that contextual oppositions function in the same manner with teachers' identification and discussion of homophobic language and behaviors, as they relate to the school environment.

In examining how homophobic language and behaviors function within educational settings, I interviewed a group of teachers to determine how they were defining and labeling homophobic and non-homophobic words/

actions in their schools. When asked to discuss examples of homophobia most participants mentioned the use of the F word but argued that the word has other meanings not related to sexuality. They believed that some students may call someone else the F word and not be referring to his or her sexuality, but rather are making a statement similar to "You're an idiot." Because of this, most teachers acknowledged that they did not address students' use of the F word in their schools or their classrooms. As with the F word, most teachers reported that they did not address the use of the word "gay" because of the uncertainty about its meaning. A number of the teachers stated that they hear the phrase "that's so gay" quite often in their classrooms and hallways and never reprimand the students. These meanings of these phrases have evolved into "new" meanings that are antithetical of their traditional meanings.

In these incidents and discussions, theses teachers were constructing their own definitions of homophobia language through their constructions of contextual oppositions. For example, for these teachers, the F word has many different modern meanings within their students' socialized constructions of language (depending on the contextual use), yet, rarely including a derogatory slur for non-heterosexual identities. Thus, teachers are more willing to accept the use of the word in the school because the word has become a neutral word with a ubiquitous meaning. Specifically, the word acquires new meanings based on its contextual uses. In other words, for these teachers, it is acceptable to call a student the F word because there is a level of uncertainty in the meaning and use of the word. Unless the student using the word becomes physically violent with the student he or she is harassing, it is difficult to label the use of the word as homophobic (Jones, 2012).

As with the F word, these teachers construct oppositions through the use of "that's so gay" and "gay." For these teachers, "that's so gay" and "gay" do not always translate into homophobic language in all circumstances. As cited above, some of the teachers believe that "that's so gay" means "that's stupid" or another non-homophobic phrase. Therefore, as with the F word, these participants are accepting of this use of language in their classrooms because of a contextualized understanding.

To further support my postulations concerning contextualized oppositions, I would like to discuss the findings from a recent study that I conducted examining the climates of Virginia's colleges and universities, as those climates relate to non-heterosexual identities. The study involved a comprehensive anonymous survey. Participants were students, faculty, and staff of public and private (non-religiously affiliated) institutions in the Commonwealth of Virginia. Several of the questions asked participants to discuss the use of homophobic language on their individual campuses. A surprising number of respondents made statements about the use of "that's so gay" or "the F word." Although it was not surprising to know the respondents heard such language on their campuses, it was surprising to realize that most of the respondents did not believe the language was homophobic. In fact, most of the respondents made statements such as, "It is not a bad slur to gay people. When people say these phrases, they mean something is dumb, or someone is dumb." The respondents who heard these phrases and did not classify and define those phrases as homophobic slurs were indeed defining the use of the hate language based on the context of the usage and current popular culture meaning.

Although I do not deny the role of popular culture in our communities, it is important to examine how these students have removed a hatred meaning and replaced it with a popular culture meaning all based within the context of the use of the phrases. This is quite problematic because hate language has power when it is used. Although, it may mean "you're stupid" to a heterosexual student using the language or in "popular culture," it still maintains a derogatory slur for non-heterosexual identities, which can create an unpleasant environment for a non-heterosexual student who is also sitting in the classroom. Thus, the hate language perpetuates intolerance in the classroom. By placing hate language within contextual oppositions, participants imply that the word is an acceptable use of hate language. Educators may hear a student call someone the F word and will not address use of the word as a homophobic remark, because of their construction of a contextual opposition.

Yet, it is imperative to recognize the reality of hate language such as the F word. According to the Oxford English Dictionary (2008), [the F word] has had numerous meanings, such as "an odd strip of land," or "something that hangs loose," and even "a junior who does something for a senior." In the late 1800s, the word was equated with cigarettes. But, in the early 1900s, the word developed new meanings such as "men or boys who exploit sex for profit" or "a road kid with homosexual tendencies." The word later developed into a derogatory slang word for gay men, likely an abbreviated form of [the F word] (Jones, 2010).

Likewise the word "[the F word]," according to the Oxford English Dictionary (2008) began as "a bundle of sticks." In the late 1500s, the word had a "special reference to the practice of burning heretics alive." In doing so, the word became an emblem that "heretics who had recanted were obliged to wear on their sleeve, as an emblem of what they had merited" (Oxford English Dictionary, 2008). In the mid to late 1800s, the word was also applied as a derogatory word for a woman. One might say, "that old [the F word] Mrs. Riordan" (OED, 2008). Yet, around 1914, the word became a demeaning slur for gay men. For example, the Oxford English Dictionary cites the following: "All the [the F word]s (sissies) will be dressed in drag at the ball tonight," and "Duffy was no queen, no platinum-dyed freak, no screaming [the F word]" (Jones, 2010, p. 20). The word has other numerous derogatory meanings related to non-heterosexual identities.

In this chapter, I argue that educators define, discuss, and label homophobia through the contextual use of language. These contextual oppositions became the process through which educators develop their definitions and understandings about homophobia in their school communities. As a result, these oppositions influence how these teachers interpret language and label that language as homophobic or non-homophobic. This is problematic because allowing educators to continue to define homophobia in terms of contextual oppositions, allows them the opportunity to not view all hate language and behaviors as inappropriate. In doing so, teachers affirm some hate language/behaviors and reject other hate language based on social constructions and contextuality.

By not addressing all hate language equally it suggests a level of socially covert heterocentricity. By allowing these phrases to exist in classrooms and schools, teachers are, knowingly or unknowingly, perpetuating and engaging in heteronormative practices. Thus, they are inadvertently engaging in homophobia. By allowing these phrases to be repeated, and in many cases deemed as acceptable, these teachers are allowing homophobia to continue, without being labeled as overtly homophobic. Therefore, these teachers are inadvertently perpetuating homophobia and heterosexism through their constructions of contextual oppositions.

In order to begin unnormalizing education, we must begin treating all homophobic language in the same manner. For some, the phrase, "that's so gay" or the F word may not be harmful because of how it is used and by whom, but it is harmful if one happens to be non-heterosexual. Thus, as educators we must begin to dismantle contextual oppositions, so that all hate language, regardless of its contextual use, is not tolerated in schools and classrooms. If a student says, "that's so gay" or the F word, he or she should be reprimanded in an appropriate manner. In doing so, teachers are destroying the hierarchy and opposition that exist in their conceptualization of hate language. By doing so, teachers send a message to students that all hate language is unacceptable in his or her classroom. Therefore, creating an educational environment where educators are not only dismantling their own conceptual oppositions but also those of their students.

CHAPTER 6

(UN)DERSTANDING THE ROLE OF MULTICULTURAL EDUCATION IN ADDRESSING HOMOPHOBIA IN SCHOOLS

I have colleagues who do not have a clear understanding of multicultural education.

—Cindy, an elementary teacher

In order to unnormalize education, it is imperative to conceptualize the role of multicultural education and its impacts on educational environments. For the purpose of this discussion, I use a definition of multiculturalism as the process of creating acceptance of multiple cultures within educational settings. Through the process of multiculturalism, individuals are able to express their own culture without the fear of rejection and intolerance (McLaren, 1995). Further, as Asante (2007) states, "multiculturalism in education is the quality of creating and sustaining curricula, academic activities, programs, and projects that actively enhance respect for all human cultures" (p. 1). Further, Neito (1992) defines multicultural education as

> the process of comprehensive school reform and basic education for all students. It challenges and rejects racism and other forms of discrimination in

(Un)normalizing Education:
Addressing Homophobia in Higher Education and K–12 Schools, pp. 37–42

schools and society and accepts and affirms the pluralism (ethnic, racial, linguistic, religious, economic, and gender among others) that students, their communities, and teachers represent. (p. 208)

In exploring multiculturalism as it relates to homophobia, I posit that multiculturalism is a viable tool in combatting homophobia in educational environments.

Multiculturalism can be traced to the Civil Rights Movement (McLaren & Sleeter, 2000). According to McLaren and Sleeter (2000), "African-American scholars and educators, working in conjunction with the Civil Rights Movement as a whole, provided much of the leadership of multicultural education" (p. 16). Originally, the term "multiethnic education" was used to address issues surrounding race and race relations. "Multicultural education" was used later to include other areas of diversity, including gender, and sexuality. In fact, "culture" became a part of multicultural education to entice the audiences of the White educators who believed that the movement was not embracing all cultures (McLaren & Sleeter, 2000). Also during the development of multicultural education, Title IX became a part of educational institutions. Title IX was enacted in 1972 as a federal law that prohibits any educational program that receives federal funding to deny the participation of someone based on biological sex. Title IX became a catalyst that helped White middle class educators embrace multiculturalism because it now included issues of sexism. Through the progression of history and the gay rights movement, multiculturalism embraced queer culture, as I discuss later in this section (McLaren & Sleeter, 2000).

In addition because of its roots in the Civil Rights Movement, multicultural education became a part of college accreditation processes. Specifically, multiculturalism became an official part of colleges of education in 1979 when the National Council for Accreditation of Teacher Education (NCATE) programs added multiculturalism to its list of requirements for accreditation to address all areas of cultural differences in teacher preparation (Messner, 1994). NCATE requires that teachers must be committed to cultural diversity in all areas of education. Such a commitment begins with the education of the pre-service teachers (Messner, 1994).

In discussing race and oppression, multiculturalism became an avenue for colleges of education to begin to think about the struggles of power and language through educating pre-service teachers. Through colleges of education, pre-service teachers learned about different cultures and how to incorporate cultural diversity into their classrooms. Because of teacher education programs, cultural diversity became an attribute of multicultural education. McLaren (1995) suggests that multiculturalism became a way for students and teachers to validate other cultures within classrooms through pedagogical practices. Bedford (2002) argues that multiculturalism enables individuals to live and work in places that cherish diversity of all types. Moreover, one aim of multicultural education was to ensure that students' different cultures are understood in the classroom and school. Indeed, Gay (2007) argues that multicultural education should provide tolerant places where students feel validated so that they can engage in learning. Therefore, multiculturalism became a philosophy that embraces the importance and the legitimacy of cultural diversity (Gay, 2007).

In acknowledging and accepting different cultures, multiculturalism provided a foundation for a reform movement to change school atmospheres through including the idea of cultural pluralism within multicultural practices. Cultural pluralism, as Grant (2007) suggests, is the idea that there is no one dominant culture that defines what it means to be an American. Cultural pluralism thereby redistributes power from the dominant culture and away from Eurocentrism (Grant, 2007). The constituents of cultural pluralism are grounded in the concepts of respect for all individuals, acceptance of differences among cultures, and understanding other cultures (Baptiste, 1979). Because of cultural pluralism, multiculturalism in schools became a philosophy that involved more than the content taught but included policies and pedagogical methodologies (Bennett, 2003). For example, schools began to examine several core principles including teaching about the influence of stereotypes about different cultures, values that are shared among cultures (justice, freedom, peace), and how to interact with others from different cultures (Banks et al., 2001).

In addition to the notions mentioned above, Banks et al. (2001) also argue that one of the main purposes of multicultural education is to provide places where different social and culture groups can interact without fear. Because of this belief, multiculturalism became a catalyst that promoted tolerance and safety for GLBT students by educating teachers about the GLBT culture. In order to educate teachers about GLBT culture, one must first understand the reality of an existing GLBT culture. GLBT culture, or queer culture, is a shared set of beliefs and acknowledgments among the gay, lesbian, bisexual and transgender community (Tierney, 1997). It is a culture that maintains a history of oppression and hatred, civil rights, and community activism. According to Nowlan (2007), queer culture can be traced throughout history, including events such as the Stonewall Riots, the AIDS epidemic, and the modern gay rights movement. In addition to the historical aspect of culture, Nowlan (2007) argues that GLBT individuals live and function within a community that has established a distinct culture with contributions to literature, art, film, history, and language. It is a culture that maintains a set of practices and belief systems that one must navigate in order to function within GLBT community (Tierney, 1997). Such practices can be as simple as understanding that gay men who are in committed relationships may choose to wear wedding bands on their right hand, instead of the left hand. Beyond acknowledging the GLBTQ culture, Letts (2002) suggests that adding sexual diversity to teacher education programs through multiculturalism helps to make visible lives of gay and lesbian students. It prepares teachers to deal with sexual differences in the same manner that it prepares teachers to address differences in race, class, and gender.

Other scholars also believe that multiculturalism is the key in constructing tolerant educational settings for GLBTQ students. Mathinson (1998) suggests that in order for gay and lesbian students' culture to be validated by schools, teachers need to learn appropriate ways to integrate GLBTQ culture into classrooms, which can be done through multiculturalism. Kumashiro (2004) suggests that for teachers seeking concrete methods for addressing homophobia in their schools anti-oppressive education[1] and multiculturalism may be viable tools. Further, in addressing the GLBT issues in classrooms, Asher (2008) argues that multicultural education can destroy the oppressive nature of binaries such as self and other, queer and straight. In doing so, teachers must work against the oppression that exists within society (Kumashiro, 1999). Thus, multiculturalism is an appropriate method to address GLBTQ culture within educational environments, in doing so it becomes an appropriate avenue to address homophobia and homophobic behaviors.

However, there are challenges to implementing multicultural education into educational environments. One challenge involves faculty and staff professional development. Specifically, a majority of faculty members are not trained in multicultural education; thus, the lack of training and knowledge of multicultural education is problematic when attempting to address issues of homophobia on campuses. For example, Stallworth, Gibbons, and Fauber (2006) discovered faculty's knowledge concerning multicultural education restricted their own educational choices. Thus, it is naïve to believe change can occur without proper faculty and staff professional development exploring multicultural education.

Secondly, I posit there are negative beliefs concerning multicultural education within educational settings. Specifically, I have spoken to several directors of multicultural centers on college campuses who propose a lack of investment from faculty, staff, and administration on their campuses. In an interview with one director, he stated, "When I came to campus, I thought this campus would be different. But, it is like every other campus I have worked at. It is very difficult to get people to buy into the idea of multiculturalism. It is not important enough. If it was important, there would be more support for the center and what we do."

In order to address homophobia in schools, one must focus on the individuals or institutions that hold the power and examine why those institutions are allowing heterocentricity to continue. Multiculturalism seeks to address hegemony through elucidating how dominant cultures control society. In doing so, the main focus of multiculturalism is to show how hegemony functions in society in relation to cultures (Asante, 2007). Thus, to create change in schools, Banks (2006) argues that all educational levels should be "substantially reformed and educators must acquire new knowledge and skills" (p. xvii). Thus, multicultural education must transpire throughout the entire school environment, constructing new knowledge about non-heterosexual identities and culture. In doing so, the acknowledgement of difference must be holistically examined within an educational setting. Therefore, multicultural education must be infused into current educational environments. Individuals who learn about various cultures are capable of being more open-minded, which will help to reduce social oppression in schools, and by extension the larger community and society. As Gay (1994) writes, "All ethnic, racial, social, and cultural groups in the United States have been, and are, instrumental in shaping its history, life and culture" (p. 109). Therefore, As Neito (1992) postulates, educational leaders must challenge intolerance; so that our students can develop into culturally accepting citizens.

Thus, I postulate the role of multicultural education is paramount in addressing homophobia in schools. Specifically, multiculturalism must be infused into all academic environments. For K–12 environments, all faculty, administrators and staff must engage in professional development opportunities to help them conceptualize how multicultural education can influence the level of tolerance in their school buildings. Further, administrators at all levels must begin mandating multicultural awareness beyond engaging with culture foods on certain cultural holidays. Multiculturalism must be incorporated into the daily lives of the school building. For example, multicultural literatures should be utilized at all grade levels when appropriate. Moreover, other multicultural curriculum should be added to the current mandated curriculum. Specifically, educators could discuss the importance of different cultures in the development of a scientific theory or within mathematics.

For the collegiate level, I argue the physical representations of multicultural centers should be examined because the initial impression of multicultural centers may indicate a belief that multicultural centers and college administrators are concerned more with racial diversity, rather than, a truly inclusive notion of diversity. Specifically, I searched over 100 college and university multicultural/diversity center websites. A vast majority of those colleges' websites had overwhelmingly African American leaders in the diversity center. After discussing my discovery with a Director of Diversity with a large state institution (who is African American), he responded,

I am a little shocked that more of the directors are not African American. In the realm of diversity education, most colleges view diversity as racial diversity. Colleges tend to not embrace a truly inclusive model of diversity. It is also about appearances. We want people outside of the college to see that our diversity endeavors are led by an African American. There are amazing Caucasian Females among others who are doing great things in diversity education, yet, the face of our diversity programs and centers are mostly African American. It is a shame that we are still caught on a traditional model of diversity.

Thus, I argue collegiate environments should more adamantly address how the college community and the outside community view their diversity endeavors. In doing so, adopting a more inclusive definition and "face" of diversity for the community to view may impact the perceptions of others concerning the university's stance against homophobia and tolerance towards GLBTQ individuals.

Multiculturalism embraces the notions of tolerance and acceptance of all cultures. Therefore, if educational settings would embrace and perpetuate the attributes of multicultural education, which should include GLBTQ culture and belief systems, then the possibilities of creating safe schools for non-heterosexual identities would improve. Multiculturalism can be the catalyst to help school officials at all levels begin grappling with the ways through which issues of sexual identity are examined, discussed, and implemented in their educational communities.

NOTE

1. According to the Center for Anti-Oppressive Education, anti-oppressive education addresses the many ways through which educators can challenge the many different forms of oppression in schools. By oppression, they mean the ways that certain ways of being or identity in society are privileged over others.

CHAPTER 7

(UN)DOING UNSUPPORTIVE SCHOOLS

Of all GLBTQ students who engaged in the National School Climate Survey, "slightly more than half (53.4%) could identify six or more supportive educators and less than a fifth (18.2%) attended a school that had a comprehensive anti-bullying policy." (GLSEN, 2012)

Where is their support group?

—Fran Steigerwald, PhD, LPC

Supporting all students should be a mission of all schools and universities. However, there is a lack of support for non-heterosexual individuals in higher education and K–12 environment. Unlike racism and sexism, many non-heterosexual students do not have a strong familial support system. If an African American student is harassed because of his race, he can return home and receive some support from family. A father or mother may be able to give the student affirmation that he or she was harassed and this is what we should do. Likewise, a mother can console her daughter who may have been harassed because of her biological gender. In other words, there is a broader possibility of support from family when these other "isms" take place within schools.

With non-heterosexual students, the parental support system may not be a viable option. In many cases, the student may not be out to his or

(Un)normalizing Education:
Addressing Homophobia in Higher Education and K–12 Schools, pp. 43–52
Copyright © 2014 by Information Age Publishing
43

her parents. For many non-heterosexual students, he or she may not want to share with his father how he or she was harassed in school. Thus, the support systems necessary for non-heterosexual students primarily reside within schools. To that end, supportive schools are important in the process of creating safe and affirming schools for non-heterosexual individuals.

As a professor in a teacher education preparation program, I, along with my colleagues believe quite strongly about the importance of preparing our students to create supportive and tolerant classrooms. For our institution, as with other teacher preparation programs, we use multicultural education as the framework for completing this task. As discussed in the previous chapter, multiculturalism is the process of creating acceptance of multiple cultures within educational settings. Through the process of multiculturalism, individuals are able to express their own culture without the fear of rejection and intolerance (McLaren, 1995). Asante (2007) states, "multiculturalism in education is the quality of creating and sustaining curricula, academic activities, programs, and projects that actively enhance respect for all human cultures" (p. 1). In exploring multiculturalism as it relates to homophobia, I posit that multiculturalism is a viable avenue to create supportive classrooms for non-heterosexual identities. However, a number of teachers and administrators are not embracing multicultural education. For example, in one discussion with a teacher, I learned a majority of teachers simply do not have time to construct truly multicultural classrooms because of the "chaos of the other things that we have to do." The teacher later stated, "I have colleagues who do not have a clear understanding of multicultural education."

Thus, one avenue for undoing unsupportive schools is to mandate multicultural education training for all educators and staff. Multicultural education is important because it requires a level of self-reflection and self-awareness. It requires individuals to conceptualize their own culture and how their own biases about other cultures and belief systems have been socially constructed. In doing so, multicultural education helps dismantle the binary constructions of the importance of the dominant culture over other cultures; thereby, viewing each culture with respect and equality.

CURRICULUM

In addition to applying the principles of multiculturalism, creating supportive environments involve examining and utilizing appropriate curriculum in our schools. As a former high school English teacher, I can attest to the necessity to examine the curriculum of classrooms. The English classroom can be a dynamic dialogical space to engage in discussion of difference and "otherness." With an array of literature, the possibilities are endless. Yet, in my years of teaching in the K–6 classroom and with working with K–12 educators, there are few educators who use their curriculum to address heteronormativity. Few educators mention the beliefs that Shakespeare may have been bisexual. Few teachers mention the reality of Tennessee Williams' and Truman Capote's sexuality. Yet, these are powerful places that can be utilized to begin unnormalizing education because such discussions open classroom dialogue concerning difference.

However, educators must conceptualize how curriculum engages in the process of socialization and, in doing so, classrooms create atmospheres where normative behaviors are constructed and perpetuated. In discussing curriculum, it is important to examine the role of hidden curriculum in educational settings. For the sake of this discussion, I broadly define hidden curriculum as the avenue that schools use to reinforce society's normative ideologies. In essence, institutions use hidden curriculum as a mechanism to teach students acceptable societal behaviors. Thus, hidden curriculum encompasses what students learn from their educational experience, not the blatant texts or specific objectives of lessons.

In a recent study with a graduate student (Alicia Neely), I explored the role of hidden curriculum in social studies textbooks that were currently being used in local school districts. Specifically, we examined 15 American history textbooks which were published between 2003 and 2010. In our examinations, we were seeking the extent to which non-heterosexual identities were represented in the texts. There were no specific regulations regarding how non-heterosexual identities were represented. Therefore, this representation could maintain a wide range of possibilities.

In examining hidden curriculum as it related to non-heterosexual identities, several findings emerged from the analysis. Specifically, the Stone Wall Riots and Harvey Milk, two fairly important events in the gay liberation movement, were never mentioned in the 15 textbooks that we examined. Both of these historical events took place between 1960 and 1980 during a time dubbed as the sexual revolution. Although the revolution is discussed in two of the textbooks examined, the publishers chose to concentrate on heterosexual events that took place during this era, omitting non-heterosexual identities or events (other than one photograph, which is discussed below). This finding exemplifies how curriculum perpetuates heteronormative behaviors. Specifically, the texts were published after 2000, thus; one may expect more detailed descriptions and/or discussions about this marginalized group during this time period in American history. By omitting non-heterosexual individuals' contributions to this era, these textbooks were continuing to support the normative behaviors to which schools socialize students. Specifically, this omission causes students to believe that non-heterosexual identities did not have a vital role in this time period.

Secondly, three out of the 15 texts examined discuss acquired immune deficiency syndrome (AIDS). Two of the texts linked non-heterosexuals with the disease. Specifically, one text used the term "gay disease." Although some believed that AIDS was strictly a "gay disease" when the disease was first discovered, new beliefs have emerged about the disease and how individuals acquired it. These new beliefs surfaced well before the publication of the textbook, yet they were not included in the textbook. By omitting the pertinent information from the text, the publishers are continuing to fuel the homophobia that is connected to the early era of the AIDS epidemic. In doing so, the omission leaves students the inability to disconnect the early beliefs about AIDS and gay men because students do not have the most recent scientific beliefs about the disease. This inability causes students to continue to believe what most scholars have disqualified about AIDS.

Additionally, in examining the texts, there is only one text that photographically depicts non-heterosexual identities, a photograph of a gay civil rights march in Washington, DC in 1987. The photograph is located in one of the two text's discussion of the sexual revolution. It is important to mention that there is no further discussion to support the photograph. There is simply the caption: "gay civil rights March, 1987 in Washington, DC." Most importantly, the picture depicts individuals who conform to society's stereotypes about gay men. In doing so, the textbook perpetuates stereotypes about this marginalized population, and in doing so, continues to perpetuate a binary of "us" and "other."

Homophobia is a tremendous challenge in our schools. To add to the troubling nature of homophobia, I posit that hidden curriculum is perpetuating the problem. In doing so, schools are reproducing heteronormative ideologies, which to some extent aids in creating unsafe places for non-heterosexual students and staff. Therefore, it is imperative that educators examine their own curricula for biases and hidden curriculum. Because of hidden curriculum, it is important to supplement textbook curriculum with other sources to help decrease the replication of heteronormative ideologies, and to create safe places for all students. Specifically, Banks (2010) postulates "a curriculum that focuses on the experiences of mainstream Americans and largely ignores the experiences, cultures, and histories of other ethnic, racial, cultural, and religious groups has negative consequences for both mainstream American students and students of color" (p. 229). Indeed, his belief also applies to the lives of GLBTQ students in K–12 and higher educational settings. In terms of non-heterosexual individuals, the negative impact of excluding GLTBQ curriculum hinders the creation of an authentic tolerance toward non-heterosexual identities. Therefore, as Schultz (2010) argues, such exclusion causes an educational environment where students are not "taught to think critically, create personal connections to the learning process or value the ideas of all people"

(p. 6). Thus, it is imperative educators promote different perspectives about difference and in doing so, provide a framework for discussing and exploring the positive attributes of non-heterosexual identities to the overall culture of the school and community.

Curriculum, at all levels, can create a more tolerant educational community and by extension a more tolerant society. Because a majority of students grow up in a monoculture environment that values heterosexuality, there are few first hand experiences with non-heterosexual individuals. Thus, there are few experiences in which these students are able to truly conceptualize the reality of non-heterosexual identities. In order for students to develop a tolerant belief system about GLBTQ culture, I postulate students must encounter these experiences through the curriculum utilized within their educational experiences. In doing so, students are able to "articulate the idea that each culture has valuable elements, which can coexist together and enrich each other, thus creating true cultural diversity" (Rodriguez-Valls, 2009, p. 11). The overall goal of integrating GLBTQ culture and curriculum in all levels of schooling is to eradicate the impact of homophobia and intolerance.

Thus, as educators, we must examine our curriculums for hidden biases that perpetuate homophobia and heterocentricity. Scholars argue that teachers and educators should examine the curriculum for biases when dealing with GLBT students, as educators have done with racism and other issues facing minorities. Thus, the language of school curricula perpetuates anti-gay rhetoric and shapes the way that students view non-heterosexual identities. Moreover, most curriculums do not provide opportunities to teach about same-sex relationships or to discuss sexual issues surrounding non-heterosexuality. By omitting such topics from the curriculum, it does not enable students to reflect on sexual identities. Instead, a critical curriculum can create classrooms where the "language of analysis and discussion breaks the binaries of sexuality" (McLaren, 1995, p. 119); yet many teachers use curriculum that does not address issues of sexuality because of fears of dismissal, reprisals from community and parents, general lack of awareness, or because they harbor homophobic sentiments.

Scholars (e.g., Glasgow, 2002; Kissen, 1991; Lipkin, 2002) have examined differences in instruction and materials for specific grade levels. They imply that homophobia should be addressed through age-appropriate materials and pedagogy. In the following sections, I examine various strategies for curriculum development across all levels of education as well as suggestions that researchers and educators offer for K–12 and postsecondary education.

Elementary Education

For curriculum to become a tool to combat homophobia, many educators believe that elementary education should be the starting point for addressing hate language and biases about sexual diversity (Goodman, 2005; Pinar, 2007). By discussing GLBTQ issues in the early grades, homophobia in schools may decrease as these students move through the educational system. Other scholars also believe that the lower grades are the most appropriate place to begin discussing sexual diversity. For King and Brindley (2002), the elementary curriculum should incorporate the different family structures that exist in society. They advocate that teachers use books such as *Heather Has Two Mommies* (Newman, 1989), *The Library* (Stewart, 1995), and *Daddy's Roommate* (Willhoite, 1990), which deal with themes surrounding non-heterosexual identities. By making the books the focal point of class discussions, teachers can address homophobia through questions and comments.

However, conducting such discussions can present numerous challenges. Glasgow (2002) expresses concern with adding discussions of homosexuality to the elementary curriculum. As a school administrator and a lesbian, she understands the need to create safe environments in which all students can learn. For example, she implemented a sexual diversity day at her elementary school that involved teachers volunteering to read age-appropriate texts examining sexual diversity in their classes and engage students in appropriate discussions about sexual difference. Glasgow's (2002) choice to use curriculum to teach sexual difference came at a time when the number of students of openly gay and lesbian parents began to rise. She believed that every student should feel safe and supported by their teachers and school. For her, affirming the lives of students through children's literature and having a sexual diversity day in her school became a pedagogical tool to combat homophobia. Although she had support from her school board, others such as the Christian Coalition and Pro-Family Law Center actively opposed her actions concerning implementing the reading day with petitions and student exemption forms.

For many scholars, elementary education is a viable place to begin discussing sexual diversity; however, simply adding gay and lesbian themed books to one class reading day and having a day for all teachers to discuss sexuality with their students, as Glasgow (2002) did, is only a step in the right direction. In order for homophobia and heteronormativity to decrease, it may be important for teachers to examine what is being taught on a daily basis and how it may influence the lives of GLBT students. For example, students with gay and lesbian parents need to feel validated through what is read and discussed (Glasgow, 2002). Teachers should examine the language and illustrations of texts and how they depict family structures. Furthermore, teachers should question how such depictions may influence all students' validation of their family structures (Glasgow, 2002). Because of changes in family structures, families are no longer predominantly composed of a male and female of the same race; thus, it is important that teachers begin to examine the myths their texts perpetuates (Glasgow, 2002). Furthermore, Glasgow (2002) points out that teachers are often not ready to defend their curriculum choices to parents, and thus need to be trained in how to deal with community and organizational opposition to teaching about sexual diversity.

SECONDARY EDUCATION

Some secondary educators are also seeking to decrease heteronormativity through instructional strategies. However, there is considerable difference among the levels of curriculum change within the secondary environment. In the opinions of many scholars who address homophobia, the secondary level curriculum should include texts that focus explicitly on issues surrounding non-heterosexual identities. For example, some scholars suggest adding discussions to history classes about social forces and events, such as the gay liberation movement and the Stonewall Riots as an appropriate method for combating antigay rhetoric. Likewise, others argue for the inclusion of gay and lesbian literature in the English classroom, thereby engaging students in reflecting on the lives of gay and lesbian authors and characters. In doing so, all students should be required to read gay and lesbian texts, just as all students are required to read Shakespeare or other canonical authors. Such an approach provides gay and lesbian students a sense of validation for their sexual identity. Moreover, it offers an environment where students can discuss issues related to same sex relationships, sexuality, and homophobia.

Additionally, many scholars believe that teachers should capitalize on teachable moments, such as antigay remarks, television shows, and other discussion topics to challenge heterosexism by juxtaposing a remark, television program, etc., to a text that can be studied in class that deals with non-heterosexual identities. Teachable moments may include having students reflect on social justice issues, and identifying and challenging stereotypes. However, to combat possible ramifications from outside forces, the classroom discussion should be deeply grounded in the text students are reading, so that, every student feels safe. In doing so, teachers need to be aware of the feelings of all of their students, both GLBTQ and heterosexual, and how discussions may affect students' emotions.

Over the last decade, educational scholars have pushed for a change in the curriculum of schools to combat homophobia. Some advocate for explicit gay and lesbian literature to be taught in English and history class-rooms. Others maintain a less confrontational strategy by, for example, simply discussing the sexual orientation of authors, or mentioning how non-heterosexual identities were treated during the Holocaust. However, for many teachers, countering the societal hegemony about sexuality can be dangerous because such actions may affect their employment; thus, teachers who fear for their jobs may not be willing to teach explicit gay and lesbian literature or discuss gay and lesbian issues. Furthermore, without proper training, teachers may not be comfortable teaching gay and lesbian issues. Therefore, instructional strategies and curriculum development must be linked to teacher education programs and professional develop-ment.

POSTSECONDARY EDUCATION

Finally, scholars in postsecondary environments are also addressing the problem of homophobia through curriculum and instructional strategies. Proponents for curriculum change on postsecondary campuses suggest avenues such as lectures by visiting GLBT scholars, incorporating GLBTQ texts into all disciplines, and using creative writing in English class-rooms. Some argue that issues facing GLBTQ students should be formally addressed across the curriculum of each discipline on campus, which could be as simple as a guest speaker exploring how homophobia influences GLBTQ students' college experiences.

Additionally, college English classrooms are becoming a key place where homophobia and the marginalization of the GLBTQ community are being addressed through pedagogy and curriculum. A number of postsecond-ary educational institutions are offering writing classes specifically for gay and lesbian students to write about their lives and topics related to sexual diversity.

Although many scholars believe that curriculum is the key to combat-ing homophobia within school settings, beliefs among scholars in using curriculum and instructional strategies differ widely among disciplines and academic settings. For some, simply adding gay and lesbian texts to the curriculum is an appropriate method, while for others, implementing school-wide sexual diversity discussions is the best avenue to approach this problem.

Curriculum is an incredible catalyst that should be utilized to address homophobia and heteronormativity across educational levels. In order to unnormalize education, we must begin conceptualizing how curriculum impacts our students in both negative and positive manners. In doing so, we will be able to decrease the negative aspects and create safe and affirming places for all of our students.

PRACTICAL ASPECTS TO CONSIDER

Aside from multiculturalism and curriculum, there are some practical aspects to consider when creating supportive environments. One such practical support mechanism is a gay straight alliance (GSA). GSAs play a tremendous role in supporting GLBTQ students on campuses. Moreover, recent laws have been passed on a national level that deters school officials from hindering students in schools to organize a GSA. Yet, "less than a half of LGBTQ students reported having a Gay-Straight Alliance at school" (GLSEN, 2012).

In a recent interview with Fran Steigerwald, PhD, LPC, she advocates for the inclusion of GSAs on every campus. For her, GSAs provide a social and emotional support system for GLBTQ students, who may not receive support from family and friends outside of the school building. Also, the organization provides an avenue to interact with others who may share the same experiences, related to one's sexual identity. She also believes such organizations raise awareness within the school building, which in turn can help alleviate some of homophobia.

Further, in a study examining the college and university climates of higher education institutions in Virginia, the data analysis revealed a strong negative correlation among the presence of a GSA and the number of homophobic hate language students heard on campus. Thus, it is plausible to believe the presence of such student organizations does impact the university climate, as it relates to non-heterosexual identities.

ANTI-BULLY CAMPAIGNS

Additionally, it is worthy to discuss the role of anti-bullying programs in creating safe and supportive places for all students, and how such programs can be catalysts to address heteronormativity. There are a number of anti-bullying programs across the country which address the challenges that bullying causes within K–12 schools. Most of the programs include some method for infusing the ideals of tolerance and acceptance of difference. Although most programs are beneficial, it is important to consider one specific program and how the program attempts to address the problem of bullying in K–12 schools from a community-wide effort.

Communities Against Bullying (CAB) is a joint endeavor developed between two college professors (for the purpose of full disclosure, I am one of those professors), a school district and the local Sherriff's Department. The program incorporates a truly community wide effort to address bullying in this school district and the community, even offering counseling support and will include a community court aspect.

The program entails a truly collaborative nature, which involves the Sherriff reading children's books to elementary students, public service announcements broadcast throughout the community, public information addressing the signs of bullying behavior and reading materials at the local public libraries. The program also includes positive reinforcement mechanisms to award students who "do the right thing" as it relates to bullying. Moreover, teachers at all grade levels are provided with professional development opportunities and curriculum opportunities to use in their individual classes. For example, elementary teachers are provided with children's books and lesson plans (if they chose to use the plans) that discuss anti-bullying themes.

In addition to these attributes, a mascot was created named Cabbie the Coyote. Cabbie visits the schools regularly and engages with students. Cabbie also wrote a children's book which explores bullying in the younger grades. The schools were provided copies of Cabbie's book. Cabbie also makes appearances at community-wide events.

I mention this program because the program utilizes mechanisms to impact the bullying epidemic from a community perspective by focusing on difference and the value difference can bring into a community. The program focuses on all types of difference, including sexual identity. Bullying, like homophobia, must be addressed through deconstructing the normative social constructions about difference and "otherness" in society. The CAB program attempts to create supportive educational environments by impacting not only the schools, but also the broader community.

Therefore, I posit creating a supportive educational environment must entail a comprehensive anti-bullying campaign; one that addresses issues related to sexual identity. Such programs provide educators, at all levels, the materials and the framework to begin unnormalizing education and to begin creating dialogical spaces to discuss non-heterosexual identities. Further, it is imperative for educators at all levels to begin exploring the role of curriculum in perpetuating heterocentricity within their educational environments. Moreover, we should also examine the support mechanisms, such as gay straight alliances, and their influence in creating safe and affirming places for non-heterosexual students.

CHAPTER 8

(UN)DERTAKING A
PERSONAL JOURNEY

I had to ask myself: Why do I believe what I believe? It's not like I woke up one day and decided, I am going to start not liking gay people.

—A Teacher in a Professional Development

Understanding where we are with our personal journeys toward creating safe environments for all of our students, cannot be accomplished without deliberate thinking about our attitudes and beliefs toward others.

—Allyson S. Linn (Jones, 2010)

As Allyson writes in the quotation above, personal journeys are important in creating truly tolerant educational environments. Those journeys cause us to enter into those difficult metacognitive spaces. Entering into those metacognitive spaces can be quite difficult. We are combatting years of socialized normative behaviors, and exploring how those behaviors formed in our own lives can be tenuous. In many ways, we are battling the hegemony that exists in schools and society. It is the same hegemony that promotes the "otherness" mentality. It is the same hegemony that perpetuates the heteronormativity that exists in schools. It is the same hegemony that must be broken in order for authentic tolerance and hopefully affirmation of difference to manifest and grow. It is difficult, yet, it must be done.

(Un)normalizing Education:
Addressing Homophobia in Higher Education and K–12 Schools, pp. 53–56

We must enter into those critical metacognitive spaces. Why? Because those spaces allow us to examine our own biases towards others, regardless of how the "others" may be different.

As an educator and researcher, I acknowledge the reality of the levels of a personal journey. Some individuals will only philosophically and mentally travel to the authentic tolerance aspect of their personal journeys; others will reach the affirmation stage, and others will never begin the journey. There is an incredible power situated within social normalization. There are countless religious, familial, and other normalizing factors that impact individual's personal views of sexual identity. Thus, it is important for individuals to recognize how social constructions of normative sexual identity truly impact their views of others and their communities, and such a journey and recognition is necessary to create safe schools for all students.

During a professional development one teacher wrote in a reflective journal, "It was not until I was forced to face my own biases about non-heterosexual students that I was able to begin to change the way I managed my classroom in regards to hate language." She continues, "Because I am a heterosexual person, I never really thought about how a GLBTQ student must feel in a room full of heterosexual privilege. It is daunting once we begin to examine our own beliefs about difference. But, self-examination is necessary." For this teacher, examining her own personal beliefs about non-heterosexuals became the catalyst that caused her to begin to recognize heterosexual privilege and how GLBT students may feel in her room. This metacognitive practice is vital if we are to begin truly creating tolerant safe places for our students.

Recently, I constructed an online professional development for practicing K–12 teachers and administrators. The online program addresses homophobia in schools and provides educators with methods to address the problem. I received an email from one teacher who engaged in the professional development. He wrote,

> I have been teaching high school social studies for 15 years. I am an assistant football coach. I am Southern Baptist and was taught homosexuality was wrong. I have three kids. One of my kids in middle school came home and told me that he was being picked on. The kids were calling him queer and other stuff. Being a high school teacher, I never really thought about this a lot. I teach in small town America. Being picked on is part of growing up. But, then I saw CNN and a kid killed himself because of this. I started thinking about what if it was my kid. I Googled some stuff and found your site. I watched the videos. It changed the way I think about this stuff. I want to say that it changed the way that I conduct class. I am purposefully paying more attention to it in my classroom and school. Do I still believe that homosexuality is wrong? Probably. But, all kids should feel safe in school. Kids are there 8 sometimes more hours a day. It is a long time to be miserable every day.

In the email, there was a distinct metacognitive process with which this teacher engaged. He went from "not thinking about it" to changing the way that he conducts class and realizing that every kid deserves to be safe. Prior to this process, he believed that "being picked on is part of growing up." This process was a personal exploration that involved his own child and his child's experiences in middle school. Further, he was able to separate religious beliefs from his professional responsibilities. For this teacher, he was able to maintain a level of professional tolerance that appears to be authentic.

In an informal conversation with a teacher (whom I will call Brad) after a presentation I conducted during a national conference, the teacher shared with me his views about my attempts to eradicate homophobic bullying. Brad shared his personal journey. His story involved a personal catalyst; his son came out to him when his son was a senior in high school. Prior to this event, the teacher describes himself as a traditional teacher and coach. He used homophobic slurs in his daily life, at times in front of students on the practice field, and often in the teacher's lounge with his colleagues. Although, he did not accept physical harm toward any of his students, he never reprimanded students for using the F word or any other homophobic slur. Although Brad did not teach in the same school district his son attended, Brad lived with the repercussions of homophobic bullying. Brad noticed his son changing and being afraid to go to school. It was a difficult time for him and his son. His son is now in college and doing extremely well. Because of these personal experiences, Brad has changed his pedagogy and coaching practices. He now addresses each negative word that is used in both settings. When asked by students why he cares, Brad responds, "Because my son is gay, and that word is not appropriate." He even has reprimanded a colleague in the teacher's lounge. He is also leading professional development workshops in his school district to address bullying. For Brad, his personal journey to creating safe and affirming schools involved a truly personal connection to the problem of homophobia.

Personal journeys are imperative in the process of unnormalizing education. In order to dismantle the normalization of sexual identity, one must first understand how he or she formed his or her own beliefs about sexual identity. To reach this goal, I posit teacher education programs must begin creating the personal journeys in the beginning processes of teacher education programs. Specifically, teacher educators must prepare students to self-examine their own socially constructed realities concerning non-heterosexual identities.

I would like to offer the following example from one of my graduate teacher education courses. In Multiculturalism in Education, I require my students to conduct an extensive self-awareness assignment. Students are told the assignment is completely confidential, and I am the only person who will read their self-assessment. The assignment requires students to explore the development of their personal views about difference. Students are required to discuss their personal background, ancestry, religious beliefs (if any), parental influence and other outside influences, as they all relate to difference and one's construction of what difference means. In this assignment, I also ask students to write a reflective piece, in which they metacognitively explore how they believe their beliefs about marginalized populations may have developed over time. In essence, the assignment is a self-study of their own experiences with socially constructed views concerning difference.

I believe this assignment is a very powerful tool that guides students through a self-reflective analysis of their beliefs about difference. It is important to note, I am not attempting to change their socially constructed views, I am only attempting to make them aware of the power of normative constructions, and how those constructions may impact their treatment of students from marginalized populations. In doing so, I believe the assignment supports the necessity for future teachers to conceptualize the role of professional tolerance in their own classrooms and schools.

Throughout the years of teaching this course and this assignment, a number of students have commented on the acknowledgement of their own personal beliefs about difference and how the self-analysis actually made them aware of a need to consciously reflect on their classroom practices. Many students were not aware of the impact their personal beliefs had on their students.

Therefore, I argue colleges of educations must incorporate a similar structure within teacher preparation programs. Teacher education programs must provide opportunities for teacher candidates to examine their own belief systems, as those belief systems relate to non-heterosexual identities. There must be academic spaces within programs to embark on a personal reflective journey. I also argue the same principles must be incorporated in professional development programs for teachers who have no desire to attend a graduate education program. A reflective journey is a necessary process in unnormalizing education.

AFTERWORD

(Un)afraid of Hope and Change

In 1978, Harvey Milk gave his famous "Hope" speech. The speech was a poignant and powerful message during an era of prejudice for the nation. It was a speech that still maintains a powerful message to modern America. In the final lines of the speech, Milk (1978) states, "You have to give them hope. Hope for a better world, hope for a better tomorrow … hope that all will be alright. Without hope, not only gays, but the blacks, the seniors, the handicapped, the us'es, the us'es will give up…. And you, and you, and you, you have to give people hope."

In the early years of my academic career, a colleague stopped by my office. She expressed her concerns about homophobic bullying in schools and expressed her beliefs in my research and work in this arena. As I reflect on that conversation, I am reminded of her final words, "the process of schooling has to change."

Indeed, she was correct. The process of schooling must change. As educators, we must begin to conceptualize the role schooling has on the socialized normative processes of our students and by extension our communities. As the kindergarten student enters into a classroom, all of the previous years of normalized identity are confirmed and further normalization takes place. The small child learns, through affirmation of his or her teacher and peers, all of the things he or she has been taught are correct. He or she learns the hatred at home toward anyone who is different than

(Un)normalizing Education:
Addressing Homophobia in Higher Education and K–12 Schools, pp. 57–58
Copyright © 2014 by Information Age Publishing
All rights of reproduction in any form reserved.

he or she is must be true. It is in the first moments, he or she is consumed with the power of hegemony and institutional power regimes.

As the child ages, the normative processes become stronger. The child learns to develop language to describe the concept of otherness and difference. This language development becomes the catalyst for descriptive understandings of the binary oppositions and how he or she fits within those categorized notions of binaries. It becomes the moment when the child learns his or her own categorized identity within those binaries.

Later, the child enters middle school and high school. In those years, the foundation of normalized behavior is solidified. He or she has now formed stable and almost permanent belief systems about otherness. Language becomes a stronger method to express his or her dominance over the other. Homophobic slurs become common language and are thrust upon a less dominant identity within the hierarchy of the binary structure, the same structure that has been utilized and formed throughout the child's entire schooling process. After the appropriate number of years, the now adult enters into the real world, with the same social belief system as his predecessors, which continues the cyclical nature of prejudice and homophobia.

At the foundation of the process of unnormalizing education lies the reality of the power of schooling. The process of schooling is so vitally important to the continued architecture of social normalization. If schools did not continue the process, the architecture would weaken and the cyclical nature of normalization would dismantle. In doing so, the very ideology of social normative belief systems would weaken.

As educators and researchers, we must begin contemplating a schooling process that creates safe and affirming school environments for all students, regardless of the categorized notion of otherness. We must begin examining how our classrooms and pedagogy are catalysts that promote intolerance. We must examine how our schools continue to perpetuate the very binary oppositions that dictate our belief systems about difference. We must begin to truly conceptualize our role in the normalizing process of all our students, no matter the grade level.

It is through this realization we will discover the ability to dismantle the power located within binary oppositions and the normalizing process of schooling. It is not an easy task. In fact, unnormalizing education is quite tedious. It involves the demystifying of years of belief systems. It involves a process of illumination that reveals the false reality of binary oppositions and otherness. It involves the unraveling of years of social hegemony.

Yet, we must do it. We must begin unnormalizing education. In doing so, we will be able to break free from the constraints of normalization. Through the process of unnormalizing education, we will be able to give hope to the marginalized individuals within our schools and by extension our community and the greater society.

BIBLIOGRAPHY

Anderson, J. (1994). School climate for gays and lesbian students and staff members. *Phi Delta Kappan, 76*(2) 151–154.

Armstrong, M. (1994). *Creating a positive educational environment for gay and lesbian adolescents: Guidelines and resources for staff development, curriculum integration, and school-based counseling services.* Dissertation: Retrieved Dec. 07, 2004, from www.eric.ed.gov

Bedford, T. (2002). Queer developments in teacher education: Addressing sexual diversity, homophobia, and heterosexism. In R. Kissen (Ed.), *Getting ready for Benjamin: Preparing teachers for sexual diversity in the classroom* (pp. 133–141). New York, NY: Rowman & Littlefield.

Blumenfeld, W. (2002). *Making colleges and universities safe for gay, lesbian bisexual, and transgender students and staff.* Retrieved December 8, 2004 from www.lgbt-campus.org/resources/making_colleges_safe.html

Britzman, D. (2000). Precocious education. In S. Talbart & S. Steinberg (Eds.), *Thinking queer: Sexuality, culture, and education* (pp. 31–59). New York, NY: Peter Lang.

Britzman, D. (1995). Is there a queer pedagogy? Or stop reading straight. *Educational Theory, 45*(2), 151–165.

Brooker, P. (1999). *A concise glossary of cultural theory.* London, England: Arnold.

Butler, J. (1999). *Gender trouble: Feminism and subversion of identities.* New York, NY: Routledge.

Butler, J. (1993). *Bodies that matter: On the discursive limits of sex.* New York, NY: Routledge

Crocco, M. (2001). *Homophobic hallways: Is anyone listening?* Paper presented at an annual AERA conference, Seattle, Washington.

Dilley, P. (1999). Queer theory: Under construction. *Journal of Qualitative Studies in Education, 12*(5), 457–472.

59

Dinshaw, C. (1995). Chaucer queer touches: A queer touches Chaucer. *Exemplaria*, 7(1) 75–92.

Deaux, K., & Kite, M. E. (1987). Thinking about gender. In B. B. Hess & M. M. Ferree (Eds.), *Analyzing gender: A handbook of Social Science Research* (pp. 92–117). Newbury Park, CA: Sage.

Derrida, J. (2001). From *Plato's pharmacy*. In V. Leitch., W. Cain, B. Finke, & B. Johnson (Eds.), *The Norton anthology of theory and criticism* (pp. 1815–1876). New York, NY: Norton and Company.

Eaton, L. (2005). *Constructing rainbow classrooms: Non-heterosexual students' journey toward safer schools.* PhD dissertation, North Carolina State University, North Carolina. Retrieved November 20, 2008, from Proquest Digital Dissertation Database.

Elsbree, A. (2002). *Disruptive pedagogies: How teacher educators disrupt homophobia.* Paper presented at AERA conference, Madison.

Ferrero, E. (2004). *ACLU files federal lawsuit against Alabama school district.* Retrieved February 20, 2005, from http://gaymontgomery.com.

Fifield, S., & Swain, H. (2002). Heteronormativity and common sense in science (teacher) education. In R. Kissen (Ed.), *Getting ready for Benjamin: Preparing teachers for sexual diversity in the classroom* (pp. 177– 190). New York, NY: Rowman & Littlefield.

Foucault, M. (1978). *The history of sexuality.* New York, NY: Vintage.

Fullan, M. (2004). Coordinating top-down, bottom-up strategies for educational reform. *Systemic Reform: Perspecitives on Personalizing Education, 32,* 214–225.

Gallup Poll (2004). *Americans views of homosexuality poll.* Retrieved February 20, 2005, from http://www.gallup.com

Gamson, J. (2002). Sexualities, queer theory and qualitative research. In N Denzin & Y. Lincoln (Eds.), *Handbook of qualitative research* (pp 347–365). Thousand Oaks, CA: Sage.

Glasgow, K. (2002). I'm every woman: Multiple identities as part of the diversity curriculum. In R. Kissen (Ed.), *Getting ready for Benjamin: Preparing teachers for sexual diversity in the classroom* (pp. 227–233). New York, NY: Rowman & Littlefield.

GLSEN. (2003). *2003 National School Climate Survey.* Retrieved December 6, 2004, from http://www.glsen.org.

GLSEN. (2007) *Research Involving GLBT Students.* Retrieved October 5, 2007, from http://www.glsen.org.

GLSEN. (2008) *Research Involving GLBT Students.* Retrieved November 22, 2008, from http://www.glsen.org.

Godrej, F. (2003, April 3–5). *Spaces for counter-narratives: The phenomenology of reclamation.* Paper Prepared for the Midwest Political Science Association Meeting, Chicago, IL.

Gulla, A. (1999). *Textual orientations: Gay and lesbian students and the making of communities.* Paper presented at the Biennial Conference of International Federation for Teachers of English, Warwick, England.

Harbeck, K. (1995) Invisible no more: Addressing the needs of lesbian, gay and bisexual youth and their advocates. In G. Unks (Ed.), *The gay teen* (pp. 125–133). New York, NY: Routledge.

Hirt, J., Schellenberg, E., & Sears, A. (1999). Attitudes among homosexuality at a Canadian University. *Sex Roles: Journal of Research*, *3*(22), 37–58.

Hoffner-Brodsky, M., & Hoffner-Brodsky, D. (2002). Afterword: A word about getting ready for Benjamin and his two mommies. In R. Kissen (Ed.), *Getting ready for Benjamin: Preparing teachers for sexual diversity in the classroom* (pp. 13–27). New York: Rowman & Littlefield.

Human Rights Campaign. (2004). Gay marriage in America. Retrieved February 20, 2005, from http://hrc.org

Jackson, J (2001). *Come out, come out wherever you are: A synthesis of queer research in education.* Paper presented at the AERA national conference. Seattle, WA.

Jarraway, D. (2002). Tales of the city: Marginality, community, and the problem of gay identity in Wallace Thurman's "Harlem" fiction. *College English*, *65*(1), 36–52.

Jones, J. (2014). Purple boas, lesbian affection, and John Deere hats: Teacher educators' role in addressing homophobia in secondary schools. *Journal of Teacher Education and Practice*.

Jones, J. (2012). *Bullying in schools: A professional development for educators.* California: Smashwords.

Jones, J. (2011a). *Beyond the silence.* Teaching4Reform Films.

Jones, J. (2011b). *Contagious tolerance: Creating safe schools for our students.* ED518813.

Jones, J. (2011c). When school leaders are in denial: The role of teacher education programs in preparing teachers to combat homophobia. *Teacher Education Journal of South Carolina.*

Jones, J. (2010). *Making safe places unsafe: A discussion of homophobia with teachers.* Kendall Hunt: Iowa

Jung, P., & Smith, R. (1993). *Heterosexism: An ethical challenge.* Albany, NY: SUNY Press.

King, J., & Brindley, R. (2002). Teacher educators and the multicultural closet: The impact of gay and lesbian content on an undergraduate teacher education seminar. In R. Kissen (Ed.), *Getting ready for Benjamin: Preparing teachers for sexual diversity in the classroom* (pp. 201–214). New York, NY: Rowman & Littlefield.

Kissen, R. (1991, Nov. 22–27). *Listening to gay and lesbian teenagers.* Paper presented at the annual meeting of the National Council of Teachers of English, Seattle, WA.

Kluth, P., & Colleary, K. (2002). Talking about inclusion like it's for everyone: Sexual diversity and the inclusive schooling movement. In R. Kissen (Ed.), *Getting ready for Benjamin: Preparing teachers for sexual diversity in the classroom* (pp. 105–118). New York, NY: Rowman & Littlefield.

Leitch, V., Cain, W., Finke, L., Johnson, B., McGowan, J., & Williams, J. (2001). (Eds.), *The Norton Anthology of Theory and Criticism.* New York, NY: Norton and Company

Letts, W. (2002). Revisioning multiculturalism in teacher education: Isn't it queer? In R. Kissen (Ed.), *Getting ready for Benjamin: Preparing teachers for sexual diversity in the classroom* (pp. 119–131). New York, NY: Rowman & Littlefield.

Lipkin, A. (2002). The challenges of gay topics in teacher education: Politics, content and pedagogy. In R. Kissen (Ed.), *Getting ready for Benjamin: Preparing teachers for sexual diversity in the classroom* (pp. 13–27). New York, NY: Rowman & Littlefield.

Marinoble, R. (1998). Homosexuality: A blind spot in the school mirror. *Professional School Counseling, 1*(3) 4–8.

McLaren, P. (1995) Moral panic, schooling and gay identity. In G. Unks (Ed.), *The gay teen* (pp. 119–131). New York, NY: Routledge.

Merkle, D. (1997). *Inclusive science education: What does it look like? Confronting homophobia and providing equity for homosexuals in our science classrooms.* Paper presented at the annual meeting of Association for the Education of Teachers in Science, Cincinnati, OH.

Mesner, K. (1994). *Multicultural infusion in teacher education: Teacher educator voices.* ERIC Document: ED 380444.

Middleton, M., & Young, A. (2002). Gay ghetto in the geography textbooks. In R. Kissen (Ed.), *Getting ready for Benjamin: Preparing teachers for sexual diversity in the classroom* (pp. 91–102). New York, NY: Rowman & Littlefield.

Newman, L. (1989). *Heather has two mommies.* Los Angeles, CA: Alyson Publications

Nowlan, B. (2008). Lectures: Introduction to critical theory and gender. Retrieved November, 15, 2008, from http:www.uwec.edu/ranowlan/theory_teaching on

A., O'Conner. (1995). Who gets called queer in school? Lesbian, gay and bisexual teenagers, homophobia and high school. In. G. Unks (Ed.), *The gay teen* (pp. 95–101). New York, NY: Routledge.

OED. (2008). *Oxford English Dictionary Online.* Retrieved from http://www.oed.com

Rofes, E. (2002). I was afraid he would label me gay if I stood up for gays: The experience of lesbian and gay elementary education credential candidates at a rural state university. In R. Kissen (Ed.), *Getting ready for Benjamin: Preparing teachers for sexual diversity in the classroom* (pp. 191–200). New York, NY: Rowman & Littlefield.

Rowse, A. (1977). *Homosexuals in history: A study of ambivalence in society, literature, and the arts.* New York, NY: Dorset.

Salih, S. (2006). *Judith Butler: Essential guides for literary studies.* New York, NY: Routledge.

Sanlo, R. (2002). Campus dyke meets teacher education: A marriage made in social justice heaven. In R. Kissen (Ed.), *Getting ready for Benjamin: Preparing teachers for sexual diversity in the classroom* (pp. 235–248). New York, NY: Rowman & Littlefield.

Sears, J. (1992). Educators, homosexuality and homosexual students: Are personal feelings related to professional beliefs. In K. Harbeck (Ed.), *Coming out of the classroom closet: Gay and lesbian students, teachers and curricula* (pp. 150–175). Binghamton, NY: Harrington Park Press.

Sedgwick, E. (1993). *Tendencies.* Durham: Duke University Press.

Sedgwick, E. (2001) *Epistemology of the closet.* Los Angeles, CA: University of California Press.

Smith, L. (1989). *Writers who are gay and lesbian adolescents: The impact of social context.* Paper presented at the annual AERA conference, Los Angeles, CA

Spurlin, W. (2002). Theorizing queer pedagogy in English studies after 1990. *College English, 65*(1) 9–16.

Stewart, S. (1995). *The library.* New York, NY: Farrar, Straus, Giroux.

Straut, D., & Sapon-Shevin, M. (2002). "But no one in the class is gay": Countering invisibility and creating allies in teacher education programs. In R. Kissen (Ed.), *Getting ready for Benjamin: Preparing teachers for sexual diversity in the classroom* (pp. 29–41). New York, NY: Rowman & Littlefield.

Sumara, D. (1997). Queer theory and literacy education. *English Quarterly, 33*(3) 14–17.

Tierney, W. (1997). *Academic outlaws: Queer theory and cultural studies in the academy.* Thousand Oaks: SAGE.

Tierney, W., & Rhoads, R. (1993). Enhancing academic communities for lesbian, gay and bisexual faculty. *New Directions for Teaching and Learning, 53*(1) 43–50.

Underwood, J. (1998). Young, female, and gay: Lesbian students and the school environment. *Professional School Counseling, 1*(3) 15–21.

Unks. G. (1995). Thinking about the gay teen. In. G. Unks (Ed.), *The gay teen* (pp. 3–12). New York, NY: Routledge.

Uriber, V. (1995). Project 10. In G. Unks (Ed.), *The gay teen* (pp. 203–210). New York, NY: Routledge.

Uribe, V., & Harbeck, K. (1991). Addressing the needs of gay, lesbian, and bisexual youth. *Journal of Homosexuality, 22*(1) 9–28.

Wallace, D. (2002). Out in the academy: Heterosexism, invisibility and double Consciousness. *College English, 65*(1) 53–66.

Walling, D. (1996). *Open lives, safe schools: Addressing gay and lesbian issues in education.* Bloomfield, IN: Phi Delta Kappa Educational Foundation.

Whitney, B. (1998). Gender role variables and attitudes towards homosexuality. *Journal of Sex Roles, 45,* 691–721.

Willhoite, M. (1990). *Daddy's roommate.* Boston, MA: Alyson.

Zeikowitz, R. (2003). Befriending the medieval queer: A pedagogy for literature classes. *College English, 65*(1) 67–80.

ABOUT THE AUTHOR

Joseph R. Jones, PhD is a former high school English teacher. His PhD is from The University of Rochester (Rochester, NY) and examined teachers' perceptions of homophobia through a collaborative professional development program. His work has been accepted at numerous national and international conferences. He has published widely on topics addressing how hegemonic masculinity impacts schools, how teachers can use media literacy to address homophobia, and how teachers address hate language differently in their classrooms, among other topics. In November of 2010, his book, *Making Safe Places Unsafe: A Discussion of Homophobia with Teachers* was released. He has been interviewed extensively by media outlets about homophobia and bullying in schools. His most recent book, *Bullying in Schools: A Professional Development for Educators,* was released in the Fall of 2012. He is currently working on a new book, *Pencils, Books and Rainbows: Educators' Experiences With Homophobia in Schools.* The book explores the problem of homophobia in K–12 schools from educators' perspectives. More recently, he has constructed a K–12 anti-bullying program with an academic colleague. He currently teaches at Mercer University.